BEN J1

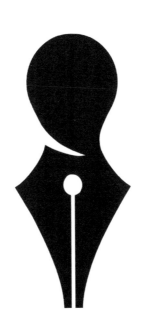

GHOSTWRITING
novels

a guide for ghostwriters and the ghostwritten

Cover design by Liz Carter (https://emcarter.carterclan.me.uk/?page_id=146).

Cover image from Shutterstock.

Interior designed and typeset by Ben Jeapes.

ISBN 978-1-0686830-0-8

www.benjeapes.com

Table of Contents

For Ghostwriters

For Everyone

Appendices

GHOSTWRITING NOVELS

Foreword

It's that line at the end where Ben shares his writing story that says it all: Ghostwriting is no one's Plan A. I'm not sure this profession will ever be included in the obligatory 'what do you want to do when you leave school?' list.

But it should be.

Ghostwriting is challenging, tiring, frustrating… and a lot of fun. If you're reading this, you are about to embark on a short journey through the world of ghostwriting, either as a potential client-author or as an actual ghostwriter. It may be entirely new territory for you or just a helpful reminder as to what is needed. Either way, the journey is worth taking.

Ben Jeapes writes from experience. And he writes well. Of course he does. There's a good deal of wisdom, a lot of helpful ideas, significant doses of common sense and bags of practical know-how. There's humour too, often of the self-deprecating kind. And of the slightly quirky British kind – apologies to non-UK readers for that!

As a fellow ghostwriter, I found I was nodding – and occasionally muttering out loud – my agreement with the words I read. This book is practical and will genuinely help you in your own journey towards a published novel. You are getting a lot for your money here. And that's the point – a short study now will save you a lot in the long term in terms of time, energy and money. But most importantly, it will help you to one day hold a book in your hands with that satisfactory glow of a job well done, a book well written, and most amazing of all, with a readership that enjoy the finished product. So there it is, that's the end game, the finished ghostwritten book – one that perhaps started out as little more than a vague idea jotted down one day on that scrap of paper you kept looking at. Until…

Happy writing.

Ralph Turner
Biographer and Ghostwriter
Leicester, UK

Introduction

The pause was just long enough to be insulting.

"She asked… you?"

I had just told my stepson about a possible new client for a ghostwriting job. The lady had been around the showbiz world for a long time, and her life had seen a lot of ups and downs, triumphs and disasters. But apart from a brief appearance on the front pages back in the eighties, when her then boyfriend was owner of one of the more important football clubs, she had never been what you would call famous. So, she was modest enough to accept that her autobiography probably wouldn't go flying off the shelves. Even so, she thought, her life might make the basis of a good novel. Reminiscences could be reshaped and remodelled, facts could be played with, libel laws could be circumvented and the result would be a cracking good read.

I agreed.

In fact, she thought that it could be a bonk-busting, fortune-earning bestseller. Something, in her own words, 'with secretions'.

Well, possibly.

And she thought that all that was needed for the riches to start flowing in was a couple of good introductory chapters, which I would write, to snag a publisher's interest.

Almost certainly not.

*

I was up for it, in principle, because it sounded fun,

but I did my best to point out the flaws in her thinking. Yes, a publisher *might* make an offer based on two brilliant chapters; that's *might* as in, it's not technically impossible. But it would be very, very unlikely. I have had unexpected breaks in my career, but none of them have had quite that level of odds stacked against them. Far more likely, at the very least, would be the publisher wanting to see the rest of the book before they made any offers. And if money ever did start flowing towards the author, it wouldn't be for another couple of years at best. Publishers do not act overnight.

There was one more thing. Money was tight and she couldn't pay me much – but we would split the profits 50-50 when they came.

'Right…,' I thought.

*

It wasn't the time to tell her the harsh truths about how profitable any book is likely to be. I'll go into these later in this book. The fact was, I liked her, I liked the thought of this project and – let's be frank – I was between projects and needed to be doing something. So, we agreed she would send me reminiscences about her life, and from those I would develop a story outline for a novel and ultimately write the first two chapters, for not much pay, which is still a greater sum (I reckoned) than zero. If she wouldn't believe me about the realities of publishing, I thought, she might believe an actual publisher when they told her. After that, I thought, we could raise the matter of a decent payment for the rest of the book.

We agreed on a deadline for me sending the chapters; she began to send me her reminiscences; I began to make notes and piece together a story structure that I thought might work. But I never got around to writing those introductory chapters because – well, because there was nothing introductory there. Nothing that would start the book with a bang. Sure, I could just start at the very beginning, describing an incident in her childhood, but that wasn't why people read novels like the one we were planning. It needed something juicy, especially given the high hopes she had vested in those two chapters. Those secretions wouldn't secrete themselves.

She began to get antsy. It had been weeks. She was dredging up painful memories. Why wasn't I writing those chapters?

Because, I can't just write chapters in a vacuum. A chapter is an integral part of a book. A book has a structure defined by the chapters within it and the way that the words and themes flow through it. Even if I'm not writing the rest of the book, I need to know where it might go after the first two chapters.

Why was I making it so complicated, she asked? Why couldn't I just write the chapters? Unfortunately, she had a friend who – wouldn't you know it – *had* had the unlikely luck I was trying to warn her against. The friend's ghostwriter had turned in a couple of chapters and (she said) riches had flowed. I didn't ask, but I was willing to bet this friend was someone quite high profile.

And it turned out that 'couldn't pay me much' did in fact mean 'couldn't pay me at all'. But the 50-50 offer on the profits still stood.

I'm a man of my word and I was still enjoying the project, so I pressed on. Perhaps not with the same sense of urgency as before, but still. Other work – paying work – did come in and I admit I let my initial deadline slip, which is something I hate doing. I eased my conscience by reminding myself she hadn't yet given me anything I could actually use.

At last, a throwaway line in one of her emails gave me the opening chapter. Her then partner had been driving them to see Genesis and – my mind boggled somewhat, but that was the point – forced her to commit a deeply intimate act on him *while he drove*. Prog rock, a fast car *and* secretions! It would have made an *excellent* opening chapter. I slotted it into the outline I had been developing, and sent it off to her for her thoughts.

But she wasn't interested. She wanted her chapters, not an outline. Too much time had passed. She said she sensed I was cooling on the project – I was politely trying to set her straight about the finances, again – and she had lost her own interest. She didn't want to do this anymore. Sorry, and goodbye.

Who This Book Is For,
And Who I Am

This lady and I both made mistakes, and I at least should have known better. By the time you finish this book you should hopefully know what those mistakes were, if you haven't already spotted them.

Remember that she wasn't aiming to write an

autobiography about her interesting life. She specifically wanted me to write a novel, and writing novels is what this book is about.

First, it's only fair of you to ask who I am, and why it's worth reading my advice. I mean, I might have just pulled it off Wikipedia, or asked ChatGPT for its thoughts.

I fell into ghostwriting by accident, but that would not have happened if I wasn't already reasonably good at what I do. If you want to know about how I became a ghostwriter, I put a longer version of my writing story in Appendix 3 (writers might enjoy it but one of my beta readers said it was too nerdy to appeal to prospective clients). I've had five novels and eighteen short stories professionally published, plus three novels self-published, plus a biography of Ada Lovelace for children which was chosen by the National Science Teaching Association as one of the Best STEM Books of 2021. That's all under my own name.

Under someone else's name I've written a lot more. As Sebastian Rook, the first three novels of *The Vampire Plagues* series published by Scholastic; as Nick Shadow, two books of Scholastic's *Midnight Library* series; and, as a variety of names that may not be disclosed, well over one million words of published fiction for clients that I also may not name.[1]

The most significant of these I call Client Zero, for the foundational role he[2] played in my career. The amount of work that I did for him gradually increased over the years to the point that I was able to give up the day job. He will

---

1   This is my response to anyone who suggests I might not be a proper writer.
2   Saying 'he' is not too much of a giveaway as it reduces Client Zero's possible identity to only half the planet's population.

pop up from time to time in the rest of this book.

I've ghostwritten both fiction and non-fiction, and I've read plenty of good advice aimed at non-fiction ghostwriters. *Ghostwriting* by Andrew Crofts, a true veteran of the art, is one book to start with; more recently, *The Complete Guide to Ghostwriting* by Teena Lyons is informative and comprehensive, and does exactly what it says on the tin. However, I found that neither of them gives ghostwriting *novels* what I think is the attention it deserves, for the very simple reason that neither author is mostly a fiction writer. I am, and as the field of fiction has some aspects that are unique to it, I think it needs a book of its own.

So, this book is for anyone thinking of hiring a ghostwriter to write a novel, and for any ghostwriter thinking of being hired. Ghostwriters, and the ghostwritten.

Defining Terms

AUTHORS, GHOSTS AND WRITERS

You might have your own notions of what each of these words means. In this book, I use them in the following senses:

- **Author:** the official author of a work – the one perhaps doing the hiring, whose name appears prominently on the front cover.
- **Ghostwriter**, or just plain **ghost**: the person hired to do the writing.
- **Writer:** anyone who writes.

BOCTAOE

'BOCTAOE' is short for 'But Of Course There Are Obvious Exceptions' and it was coined by cartoonist Scott Adams, creator of the immortal *Dilbert*, as his gift to the world. In any argument that seeks to make general points, there will always be specific exceptions that immediately come to mind without in any way invalidating what you are trying to say (like, the lady's friend who had overnight success with her ghostwriter).

I make a lot of general points in this book. For anything that seems too general, I say – BOCTAOE.

FOR THE GHOSTWRITTEN

1. What Exactly Is A Ghostwriter?

To put it simply, a ghostwriter writes so that you don't have to.

Margaret Thatcher once brought the house down at the Conservative Party Conference by lampooning Monty Python's parrot sketch, substituting the Liberal Democrats' new bird logo for the ex-avian. It made headlines and got her a standing ovation.

Of course, she did not come up with that joke. In fact she couldn't see the funny side at all. She had to be persuaded that if she just said these words, it would be funny and people would laugh. She did, it was and they did.

The joke was devised by writers, who themselves faded into the background. Because they were writing a speech, we call them speechwriters. But if they had been writing for any outlet that required reading – articles, opinion pieces, even books – then they would be ghostwriters. They were not just writing words for her to say. They were writing words in her voice, tailored to her tone and mannerisms. Apart from the bits that evince a sense of humour, it should be impossible for anyone looking at that speech to spot which bits are original Thatcher and which are her writers.

Dirty Secrets

As you will have gathered if you read my own experiences in the previous section, not all published books are written by the person whose name appears on the cover. Many are written by ghostwriters. This was once a dirty secret, and even today I get the occasional contract drafted by a lawyer that just about allows me to live on the same planet as the author, and breathe the same air as long as I don't do it too deeply, but in no other way may I be linked with their client.

Other authors are less secretive. I met an editor whose company publishes *Flying Fergus,* a series of children's books by Olympic cyclist Sir Chris Hoy about a boy and his magic bicycle. Sir Chris is apparently very open about using a ghost in his series; they even went on a publicity tour together. Perhaps it's because he is much more accustomed to being part of a team where everyone plays to their strengths. There's a lot of teamwork involved in publishing a book; I'll come to that later.

Authors might use a ghostwriter for a variety of reasons. For non-fiction, it comes as no surprise that someone may have something that they want to communicate – an interesting life, or a set of skills, perhaps – but don't have the time or ability to write a book about it. So, the ghostwriter becomes their mouthpiece. The most recently famous non-fiction ghosted book, at the time that I'm writing this, is Prince Harry's *Spare.* That book's ghostwriter, J.R. Moehringer, benefited from writing in an era when ghostwriters are more and more coming out into the open. But I will hazard a guess that even back in 1987, not many people believed Donald Trump had actually written *The Art of the Deal*.

Non-fiction usually fulfils something someone needs to know, or meets their interests. In fiction, it's a subtly different matter. The author knows that no one *needs* to read this; the best they can do is hope that people will. You read fiction for fun, enjoyment, relaxation. You read it for the author's prose, their stories, their characters. You want to inhabit the world that the author has created. You can feel an intensely personal connection with the author, even if you've never met and they don't know you exist, so there can be a genuine sense of let-down at learning they didn't write the thing. After all, if Author A's books are being written by Writer B, then why bother reading Author A's books at all? Why not just read books that are openly by Writer B?

Novels known, or suspected, to be ghostwritten are most famously attached to the names of celebrities who are better known for other things – TV personalities, actors, sportspeople. There are two possible reasons for this, and one – let's be bluntly honest – is purely commercial. Terry Pratchett once commented that bookshops holding celebrity author signings shouldn't pass comment if the author spends an inordinate amount of time reading their own book as: "It may be the first time they've seen it."[3]

The fact is that books with a celebrity name on the cover are likely to sell. Publishers want this not only because they want to stay in business, but because a good set of guaranteed sellable titles on their list can also subsidise the

---

3   He adds: "Do not offer to help them with the long words."

rest of their activities, like publishing books by people who aren't (yet) household names.

Sometimes the name comes first: the celeb's PR people are looking for ways to grow the brand, now that they've done the Netflix series and the sportswear and perfume range, and thus the novel is attached. I have no problem with this as long as what gets into the reader's hands is coherent and readable – a pleasure to read. Which, after all, is the whole purpose of reading novels.

Anyone Can Play

But, it doesn't have to be quite so cynical. A celebrity can still be a book lover, like anyone else. Their life experiences can still spark off an idea in their heads that they genuinely want to turn into a story, and they have the market presence to make it sell.

What don't they have? Perhaps time, alongside doing whatever it is that makes them famous in the first place. Perhaps the long practice that is needed to write at novel length. Perhaps an ear for dialogue and character that isn't made of tin.

Client Zero, the foundational client mentioned in the Introduction, had enjoyed the Willard Price adventure series in his youth (as had I): *African Adventure*, *Amazon Adventure*, *South Sea Adventure* and so on. That series was about a pair of American teen brothers who travel the world with their zoologist father. It featured exciting adventures and a strong ecological message, and was impeccably wholesome and moral. Client Zero wanted a modern day equivalent for his own kids. His agents were more than happy to oblige because it grew the Client Zero brand, and the publishers took him on because they knew it would sell. A win all around. All it needed was the writing.

But it doesn't have to be celebrities hiring ghostwriters. Apart from the 'being famous' bit, any of the above can apply to anyone. Anyone can have an idea that they think could work out at novel length. A situation to explore; a character to examine; a philosophy to present to the world.

Ideas I have worked with for non-celebrity clients have included:

- Foiling an innovative money laundering plot by the IRA.
- A new take on the Jack the Ripper legend.
- The accidental creation of an AI by a master cybercriminal.
- The life and career of Marshal Ney.
- 'A story of same sex love across the denominational divide in Belfast in 1980'. (That was the author's exact description and it was enough to hook me from the start, despite being neither gay nor Irish. What a challenge!)

Not all of these found a publisher and not all of these even got further than the initial development discussion, but the point is that anyone can have that idea.

Alternatively, some people have lived such an interesting life that writing an autobiography would open them up to charges of libel (see 'The Legal Side', later on in this book) – but, file off the serial numbers, change the names, present it as a novel and the problem is solved. Added to which, they are suddenly free to take as many liberties as they like with what really happened. The lady I mentioned in the Introduction falls into this category.

What it comes down to is:

→ Idea;
→ Obstacle to developing said idea into a book;
→ Hiring a ghostwriter.

Some people make a good start at doing their own writing, but then they hit a block with one of the several stages of the process that are involved in writing a book – see the section on 'How Fiction Works' for more on that. It's very easy to start writing under the first flush of inspiration, and to dry up a few pages later.

ENTER THE GHOST

For all these reasons, you might want to hire a ghostwriter.

Later, in the section 'What Goes Into Writing A Novel', I'll describe all the different people involved in getting a novel published. Even writing your own fiction is a very collaborative effort. The same goes for all the ghostwriting I have done, working with authors, their agents and their publishers.

There are a lot of cogs that must spin in the machine to get a book published. When you hire a ghostwriter you are just hiring one of these cogs – albeit quite an important one!

Not Only But Also

The typical perception of ghostwriting is that the ghost writes the book, starting at the beginning and finishing at the end. This does tend to be the case but there are variations on the theme. For a start, my involvement with Client Zero grew as the series evolved from writing to a brief, to much more involvement in the research and plotting as well as the writing. But here are some other ways I've got involved with clients:

- *Doctoring*. For whatever reason the original ghostwriter could or would not deliver what was expected of them and I have had to step in (on one occasion taking up large chunks of a previously booked holiday, with the permission of my very understanding wife).
- *Emergency ghosting*. The client had a two-book deal with a publisher and genuinely wrote the first book on their own. But then their day job took off and they didn't have time to write Book 2. I was given an unpolished first draft of the first quarter or so of Book 2, and a detailed outline of what happens next, and I took it from there.
- *Englishing* (1). There was nothing wrong with the manuscript or story per se – except that it was written by someone whose first language was not English and who needed it to sound like it was. This included colloquialisms, character names, and pointing out that no one is going to have fond childhood memories of tobogganing in Leicestershire.

- *Englishing* (2). I'm sure it was a very good manuscript when the author wrote it in their native tongue – but they then ran it through Google Translate to get the English. As well as the straight translation errors, I had to unpick an AI's notion of what constitutes good English and turn it into something that sounded like it came from a human heart.

- *Fictionising.* Non-fiction, like biographies or histories, can still require a fiction-like voice to carry the reader along. The author can provide all the research but what is needed is some narrative to link it together and put us into the heads of the characters, extrapolating thoughts and impressions that we can't actually know about, but are based on what we do know.

- *Joining.* The manuscript written by someone else was broken into two books and I had to write the linking material to give the two parts a proper ending and a beginning.

- *Modernising.* Nothing wrong with the story when it was first written ten years ago – but that was before the smartphone revolution, so it now needed all sorts of reasons why the characters couldn't just look something up or call each other.

- *Polishing.* I've been given entire manuscripts that essentially need a comb through and polishing, sometimes with me writing extra bits to link key scenes, or otherwise straightening out kinks in the narrative.

Sometimes I don't actually touch the manuscript itself:

- *Coaching*. It's not necessarily a case of just writing a book for you. You might have an idea, but feel daunted by everything else that needs doing. You might have given it a good try yourself, but it just... *doesn't*. You might just need someone else to listen, to coach, to encourage, to bounce ideas off – generally, to help you sort it out and get it down on paper (to use an old-fashioned phrase, which still sounds better than 'convert it into bytes').
- *Critiquing*. Very much as above, except that my involvement is only to report back to the author on the changes and edits and tweaks that I would recommend they do.
- *Populating*. The author was clear on the story she wanted to write: a significant summer holiday in her childhood. She had made friends but realised, as an adult, that she knew absolutely nothing about their pasts and backgrounds. So, I had to draw up profiles for a group of four boys and four girls from different backgrounds and classes in the early 1980s.

And some residual skills left over from when I had a day job:

- *Marketing and publicity*. Proper marketing is done by proper marketers, and I'm not one. Other ghosts might well have helpful marketing know-how. By the end of writing the manuscript your ghost probably knows it better than anyone else: so, they might help write the back cover blurb, and any publicity material, and anything else that might be needed to speed the book on its way into the hands of its readers.

- *Pitching.* If you're after a proper publishing deal then somehow your novel has to be pitched to a publisher. Every novel is different, but the ghost has probably been here before and can at least offer advice, even up to writing (or co-writing) a pitch that is designed to snag the publisher's attention. Hint: check if your desired publisher has submission guidelines and follow them to the letter.

- *Production* (for self-publishers only). I can get the manuscript typeset, and either liaise with the printers, or advise on setting it up for print on demand. The pages of the book you are holding are a sample of my wares. (The cover is by Liz Carter: I will be the first to admit you should probably get a proper graphic designer in.)

I would not offer to do any of the last three on their own, but they could certainly be combined with one of my other services.

Every ghost comes to this job from a different direction, so it's well worth asking – if they haven't already mentioned it – what else they might have tucked up their sleeve.

Why Publishers Believe In Ghosts

I will tell you a counter-intuitive secret about publishing. Publishers are deluged with manuscripts and the first thing they look for as they pick up the first page is an excuse not to publish it. Usually, by the end of the first page they know which way this is going to go.

Publishers like ghostwriters because they will know the manuscript has been written by a professional, and they can deal with the writer on a pro basis. Any manuscript requires editing, which entails time and expense, but a ghostwritten one will probably require less. And where changes do need to be made, they will be done in a timely manner, without the outraged author breathing fire and brimstone that anyone should dare challenge their perfect prose. (Which is rare, but does happen.)

At least, that is how it should be, and that is how I always try to act. BOCTAOE.

Ready to Make That Decision?

You might already feel able to make a decision now: should you hire a ghostwriter? However, as I'm specifically talking about ghostwriting novels, you might want to read the next couple of chapters first: 'How Fiction Works', and 'What Goes Into Writing a Novel'.

2. How Fiction Works

"There are three rules for writing the novel.
Unfortunately, no one knows what they are."
– W. Somerset Maugham.

If you're writing a novel then there is planning to do and decisions to be made, and while your ghost *could* do all of it, the more they have to do, the more you'll end up paying them and the less the finished project will feel like *your* book.

If you're already a writer and thinking of becoming a ghostwriter then you really ought to know this by now.

Where Do Stories Come from?

Lockdown was a productive time for the imagination. A lot of books were started, many more ideas were had, and a lot of those ended up in a ghostwriter being consulted. One query I saw came from a prospective client who was a doctor. His idea: 'A novel about a handsome doctor whose eyes meet those of a beautiful nurse across the operating table'.

And…

That was it.

My first reaction was to ask why it couldn't be the eyes of a beautiful lady doctor meeting those of a hunky and handsome male nurse in the same setting. That wasn't what

I told the gent, though. Instead I gave him the gist of what you're about to read here. (BOCTAOE!) All of what follows needs to be done if you are to end up with a novel with your name on it: the more you can do this on your own, the less you'll have to pay a ghostwriter. But someone is going to have to do it.

The doctor client didn't get back to me.

SOMEONE ELSE'S TOYS

Where do stories come from? Very often from other stories. You read something, which sparks off ideas in your own head. They may be as basic as "I could do better than that", or you may think of a new approach to take, or you may just want something out there that you yourself would want to read.

If you're really lucky, then you get to play with someone else's toys. Author Kate Saunders, like me, loved E. Nesbit's magical stories as a child: *Five Children and It, The Phoenix and the Carpet*, and (less famous, but in my opinion the best) *The Story of the Amulet*. And, like me, she did the maths and worked out that the boys in those books, Cyril and Robert, were exactly the right age to go and die horribly on the Western Front a few years later. My imagination at this point went more R.C. Sherriff than E. Nesbit, so it's probably as well that I never tried to write down what was in my head. Saunders, however, wrote *Five Children on the Western Front*, which is exactly the story Nesbit would have written, in the same tone and style as the originals, including the witty things that Nesbit had to say about gender and class – which probably went straight over the heads of the target audience, but not of any adults who might be reading the stories to them. She sticks to Nesbit's style and ethos and still manages to tell a moving WW1 story.

Of course, there is the small detail that if your favourite author died less than seventy years ago (the statutory interval after the author's death) then their work is still subject to copyright. You can write what you like in the privacy of your own home, but you may not distribute it; or if you do (for example, J.K. Rowling is known to be very relaxed about fans doing exactly that; other copyright holders are less forgiving) then you may not make money out of it.

This is not a problem. Change all the names, file off the serial numbers and make it your own. Fantasy writer Terry Brooks made his name with *The Sword of Shannara*, which, with the best will in the world, is essentially *Lord of the Rings*-lite. But (crucially) he mixed in enough original ideas of his own that he was able to develop a successful fantasy series out of it, with further novels that went in a very different direction.

Anthony Horowitz's teen hero Alex Rider would not exist without James Bond; James Bond would not exist without Richard Hannay… The sequence goes back, probably to tales of heroic chivalric knights, and beyond. They all build on what their predecessors did, but do it differently. There's no reason why the stories piling up in your head should not be the latest stage in your own favourite genre's evolution.

Where to Start…

Many novels don't get written because an author has an

idea, starts writing… and the novel just sort of peters out. Maybe there's a 'what-if?' idea that they want to explore, or they've had experiences that they think could be turned into a great tale, or they've met characters that are just begging for their own story. And… then what?

From the title, you won't be surprised that my first novel, *His Majesty's Starship*, was science fiction. It was ground zero for all kinds of ideas swarming about in my head, but there were two main ones. One was the idea of a Royal Navy, but in space – a Royal Space Force. How could such a thing even come to be? Another was an idea for the psychology of an alien race which is subtly different to our own, and which causes humans to make small but key mistakes in dealing with them. Among humans, the more senior you are, the more people you are given to command. With my aliens, the First Breed, it is quite the opposite. They evolved from a herd species and controlling large numbers is easy. The real challenge lies in commanding fewer and fewer individuals. Clever, eh?

Enough of me (though I will be back). Say you have an idea for a spy novel. The KGB is bankrolling its operations in western Europe through a rigged casino game in France. MI6 decides that the best way to deal with this is to send one of its best agents to France to bankrupt the game.

So, you sit down, and you bang out a story in which a British agent bankrupts a rigged casino game. It's over in a couple of thousand words and you've got the idea out of your system. That's the gist of *Casino Royale*, and if that's all Ian Fleming had done then the world would never have heard of James Bond.

As it was, Fleming knew his story needed much more.

PRODUCT MAY CONTAIN...

In fact, there are at least four ingredients to a novel that you need to concern yourself with.

- The *idea*, which sets the whole thing off.
- The *characters*. The person or people the story is about. The main character is the protagonist; not all novels have one, but let's keep it simple and assume that yours does.
- The *plot*. What do the characters do? What happens to them?
- The *writing*. This is how you express it all. The tone and character of the novel. The words, the style, the imagery; all the things that make your story unique. All the things that make it the story you want to tell.

All of these need to be dealt with when a novel is written, and the more you can do in advance of starting to write, the better. You can decide for yourself how much you can take on, how much your ghost should do, and how best to work together.

But don't think they all have to occur in this order. To paraphrase *Doctor Who*, you might think writing a novel is a strict progression of cause to effect, but actually it's more like a big ball of wibbly-wobbly... stuff.[4] The ingredients combine in dynamically varying proportions to form the novel, and they are all quite capable of curving back on

---

4   Paraphrased from 'Blink', by Steven Moffat, first broadcast 9th June 2007. If you've got five minutes you can watch the whole scene here: **https://www.youtube.com/watch?v=LakwV3P3qII**. It's a masterclass in combining humour, explanation and tension.

themselves and changing their own past. You can write the beginning, work your way to the end, and then realise you need to rewrite the beginning.

Let's go into more detail about each of them.

The Idea

I won't tell you how to have an idea. As we've seen, they can come from pretty well anywhere. But I hope I can give some useful pointers on what happens after.

My agent and I were talking about what I might write next. Out of nowhere, he pulled an idea that would eventually become my novel *H.M.S. Barabbas.* How about, he said, the further adventures of Jim Hawkins? What did Jim do after *Treasure Island*?

Hmm.

By the time I had got back home, the first chapter had written itself in my head. It doesn't answer the question but it provided a starting point. It begins: *"We buried the doctor today. The old man nearly made his century, which would not have surprised anyone who knew him..."* Sir James Hawkins, FRS, MD, morose and melancholy, sits down to pen his memoirs on the day of the funeral of his friend, mentor and father figure, Dr David Livesey. Clearly, it's many years after *Treasure Island*. So, what did he do next?

My agent had certainly snagged my interest.

In fact, he went further in our initial discussion: why not do for Jim what George Macdonald Fraser did for Flashman? Build up the story of an accidental hero, a man whose fame is accidental and whose legend is one big con?

I didn't want to do that, though. Jim has genuinely been a positive role model for generations of boys and I didn't want to take that away from Stevenson's accomplishment.

But there's no reason his fame can't be accidental.

FLAWED HERO

There is one key scene in *Treasure Island* which struck me as being open to two very different interpretations, depending on whose eyes you view it through: Dr Livesey's, or Jim's own. Jim is a captive in the pirate stronghold. Dr Livesey approaches under flag of truce. Jim has every chance to escape with him, but can't because he's given his word to remain. Livesey is very impressed at how seriously Jim keeps his word.

But, perhaps Jim simply knew the pirates had a gun on them both the whole time, and making Livesey go away was the only way to keep them both alive? Forget honour; supposing he was just motivated by sheer fear? And yet it's the good doctor's version that makes it into the written narrative. Supposing the truth burns at Jim's conscience, getting to the point where he would rather die than have Livesey know what really happened?[5]

Further thoughts:

Jim is a flawed hero – an interesting mass of contradictions. He is never quite as brave or as strong-willed as he would like to be (until it really counts, of course). He can be a self-righteous prig: on at least one occasion, the plot goes on hold as he pleads with a pirate to consider his immortal soul. (Stevenson was agnostic-verging-on-atheist

---

5   Spoiler alert: Jim does not die.

but he knew how to play to his Victorian gallery.) At the same time he can cheerfully blow the head off Israel Hands with a pair of pistols at point blank range (admittedly in self-defence) and joke about it.

Following the plot-convenient death of Jim's actual father in Chapter 3, part of the fascination is watching Jim torn between two father figures, both of whom are obviously fond of the lad and see a bit of themselves in him: Dr Livesey, upright and moral and just a teensy bit boring; and the pirate chief Long John Silver, an unrepentant murderer, wrong but wromantic. There's a lot of possibility here.

And, circling back to the original idea: what would Jim do next? He's still young, he's now rich and has a taste for adventure. He won't go back to meekly running the local inn with his mother.

One thing I was clear on was that this would not be a *Return to Treasure Island*. Nothing wrong with that in principle, if you can find a sufficiently convincing reason to do so, but Jim's almost last words in the original novel are: 'Oxen and wain-ropes would not bring me back again to that accursed island.' So, it would have to be a very convincing reason – and, frankly, I found the idea dull.[6] By the end of *Treasure Island*, Silver is out of the picture and Dr Livesey is clearly the man Jim admires most in the world. Obviously, I decided, Jim wants to learn medicine himself. He won't be able to do that in the unnamed west country

---

6   This has been ignored or overlooked by every author who has penned a sequel in which Jim returns to Treasure Island. In Andrew Motion's *Silver*, it's Jim's son and Long John Silver's daughter who go back there, which is not quite but almost the same. And Jim himself? He runs an inn.

village he lives in; he will have to go up to London. And what might happen to him on the way?

Well, that's when the further adventures begin, isn't it?

A Basic Foundation

That is one example of an idea taking hold, and providing a very basic foundation on which to build characters and plot.

The same notions still apply when you *don't* have an out-of-copyright original to jump off. You can start with your desired ending, and work backwards to how it needs to start; you can start at the beginning and work out logically what happens next to bring your novel to a conclusion; or you might find your starting idea actually turns out to be somewhere in between the beginning and the end, and you need to work outwards from it in both directions. The same principles still apply.

These processes are not necessarily linear: they may well feed back into each other as the work develops. At the start of the century, a company called Working Partners hired me to write a series called *The Vampire Plagues*.[7] I was essentially given the plot of Book 1, *London,* but I found it didn't quite work and I had to make some suggestions for what to add, which made so much sense that they were then incorporated into the series plot as a whole. I was actually consulted for the plot of Book 2, *Paris,* and for Book 3, *Mexico* we all sat down together and thrashed the plot out

---

7   The Working Partners modus operandi is to develop an idea for a children's book series, sell it to a publisher, hire an author to write it, and split the proceeds so that if they have accidentally found the new Harry Potter, everyone benefits.

over sandwiches. Some of which fed back into the writing of Book 1.

If you have an idea but are not sure what to do with it, a ghostwriter can help you bounce concepts around and watch them form some kind of shape. Note that there were certain presets in my own head that guided me: for example, not wanting Jim to be a villain or to return to that accursed island. You may have your own.

Your idea might not yet be laid out in all its glory, but you have enough to be getting on with. You need to decide how it all happens; in other words, the plot.

The Plot

Plotting a novel is usually my second least favourite part of the process, but it really is a pain barrier that has to be got through. My least favourite thing of all is staring at a blank screen when I want to be writing something, and even if I'm technically earning money for doing this, it leaves a bad taste in the mouth.

So, doing the blank screen staring-at during the plotting saves valuable time and effort later.

Remember the wibbly-wobbly quote? The plot itself should not be wibbly-wobbly; it should be linear, with a beginning, a middle and an end. You might however not want to *tell* the story in that order. Flashbacks and cutaways are established literary devices, and the narrative can be carefully ordered in any way the author likes for maximum effect; but the story itself, if you wrote a summary of it down afterwards, should proceed in a nice, straight line.

The *process* of plotting, though… Well, that can be all over the place.

TO AND FRO

It's generally good to have an ending to aim towards. From that you can work back to a preferred beginning, and there might be some key scenes along the way. However, joining those dots can be easier said than done.

> **Q:** How does the character escape from that locked room?
> **A:** Well, um, they know the trick about how to open a locked door from the other side.
> **Q:** And they just happen to know it?
> **A:** No, it was… um… when they were waiting in the station! They read it in a magazine in the waiting room! Ooh, that's much better, because it can be mentioned as a throwaway line in between their doing the crossword and reading that article on the royal family, and the reader won't realise it was significant until later.

Better go back and put it in, then…

LINEAR…

Robert Louis Stevenson came up with a fairly straightforward, linear adventure story in *Treasure Island.* It starts with the appearance of a mysterious ex-pirate at the inn where Jim Hawkins lives with his parents; it proceeds by logical stages of the discovery of a treasure map, the expedition to Treasure Island and various shenanigans with the pirates along the way; and ends with Jim's return to England, older, wiser and much richer than when he began.

For *H.M.S. Barabbas*, it was reasonably easy to do likewise. The overall aim: get Jim trained as a doctor *and* have him fall in with pirates. So: get him onto a pirate ship, with a good ship's doctor. Give him plenty of setbacks; a chance to learn medical skills; the realisation of what he has got himself into; an escape by the skin of his teeth, which does not in fact resolve the problem because the pirates are still out there; and, of course, ultimately a return to the lion's den to deal with the problem once and for all. Put him through hell, from a child-friendly perspective, and have the flames burn the rough edges off him.

With each stage written down, the question arose of how to get him to the next stage.

- He lives in the west of England and wants to get to London.
  → He takes a ship from Plymouth.
- He falls in with pirates.
  → The pirate ship is in Plymouth, masquerading as a legitimate navy ship but with a highly unorthodox private mission (there's a clue in its name).
- Somehow he gets on board…
  → How did young men get on board legitimate navy ships? The press gang.
- He meets the ship's doctor.
  → He impresses the captain with his intelligence

and very rough knowledge of medicine picked up from Dr Livesey; the captain decrees that he will assist the ship's surgeon.
- The ship's doctor is firmly against the idea.
  - → Jim must prove his competence somehow.

And so on.

Sometimes I hit a block; sometimes I felt I was cudgelling my brain knowing that Jim had to get from A to B somehow but I just couldn't see how. But one by one the blocks fell, and eventually I had a plot.

... AND WIBBLY-WOBBLY

Plotting *H.M.S. Barabbas* was pretty straightforward and the end product was not hugely different from what I had imagined all along. Another of my novels, young adult fantasy *The Teen, the Witch and the Thief* was more complicated. I wrote this by expanding a short story I had previously written, called 'The Grey People'. All his life, a man has been plagued by the Grey People, who will emerge from nowhere and steal parts of his memory. He knows what triggers their appearance: it is any created thing that he discerns (rightly or wrongly) to lack moral and spiritual commitment from its creator. A sloppy paint job. A poorly written book. A grey, bland shopping centre that has replaced a thriving community. For protection, he surrounds himself with items that have accrued life value and meaning; in fact, his best self-defence mechanism is to run an antiquarian bookshop.

The story was written for adults and I wanted the novel

to be a young adult fantasy. So, I switched the viewpoint to Ted, the bookshop's work experience lad in the story, who became my hero. He got a family and a complicated background. And then I developed it all – forwards and backwards and sideways in time from the couple of days that the original story took up. I developed the idea of the Grey People, what they might be, where they came from. I found myself making unexpected inroads into folk magic and the history of Salisbury, which was a nice development.

Unfortunately, after finishing the first draft, it became clear that the elements I had imported from the story didn't work at novel length. So, apart from a few nice turns of phrase that I was rather proud of from the original story, I deleted them all.

Since the Grey People were so central to the original idea, that may seem a bit drastic, but in fact, the world of the original story had now developed so much that it was surprisingly easy. Back stories had been introduced for the main characters. Ted had become the key in an age-old battle between ancient magicians, neither of whom are particularly pleasant but only one of whom is a homicidal psychopath bent on destroying the world. I was left with a manuscript full of gaping holes that needed to be filled with injections of New Added Plot. These introduced new elements that had to be worked back in, and which also opened up new possibilities leading to a sequel that I hadn't previously thought about. And though I say it myself, the book was much better as a result.

WORKING IN SERIES

It's even more fun if you are working with a series, building up to something over several books. The first Client Zero series was essentially four stand-alone books, with plots that were given to me. At various points throughout the plot of each book, the hero would get into life-or-death situations which he had to get himself out of. It was left to me to research Client Zero's work, work out what the hero would do, and make it happen, all without seeming to lecture the reader. And repeat, times three. It was fun but I won't deny maybe a little sameish by the time I had written the fourth book.

When the publishers got in touch about a second series, my main concern was that there needed to be an overarching story linking the whole series together. Otherwise it was just the story of one very unlucky boy whose life was in danger every time he went on holiday, and you had to wonder why he didn't just stay at home. The publishers duly came up with a story that carried across from book to book: uncovering a secret that can bring down a corrupt organisation, and doing something about it, as well as the stand-alone adventures required by each book.

For the third series, it was felt that with all the enemies our hero had made over the last eight books, it was time for a bit of payback: now they were coming for him. For the first time he had active foes. Oh, and they would also like me to introduce a previously unknown long-lost sister, who might be spun off into a series of her own; could I manage that?

That was fun, not least tackling all the challenges of just

how our hero could have had a long-lost sister he has never mentioned before, without trying to retrofit the earlier stories to fit the new narrative. (Hello, Mr Lucas.) To build up to the big reveal, the four-book series contained little clues and hints throughout. As our young hero looks through some old photo albums in Book 1, there is a throwaway mention of the fact that he was one of a pair of twins, the other having been thought to die as a baby. Hence, he very rarely thinks of her; hence, she has never been mentioned in the previous series. At the end of Book 3, we learn she might still be alive. Book 4, of course, introduces her.

To sum up: there are all kinds of ways a plot can develop, and you can have fun doing it yourself before you brief your ghostwriter. Or you can enlist their help if you're getting bogged down. It is another job that we take on.

Driving Force

There is a cliched phrase from the early days of adventure writing that probably no one actually said then, and no one would dare use nowadays: "With one bound, he was free". That is just cheating. Everything has to follow, with cause and effect. If someone escapes a deadly situation, we need to know how. If someone gets into trouble, we need to see it. If someone picks up some important information, it can't just pop into their heads.

The apple barrel scene in *Treasure Island* is key to the whole plot. It is the moment we and Jim learn that he is on a ship where the vast majority of the crew are cut-throat pirates. Without it, Jim and the other good guys would have been massacred without warning and there would have been no story to tell. At least, not the one we've come to know and love.

From a story point of view, Jim needs – somehow – to learn of the pirates' plans. Stevenson could have just had him overhear a casual conversation, but these men are professional killers, vicious and suspicious, and it is very unlikely they would have let their guard down enough to allow Jim to come within earshot. So, it has to be an accident that no one could have foreseen.

Jim is a growing lad. Growing lads like to snack. Jim fancies an apple. The apples are kept in a barrel on deck. The barrel at this late stage of the voyage is almost empty so he has to get in bodily to retrieve one. Thus he is out of sight when the pirates convene their impromptu council of war on the foredeck, but able to overhear every word.

Just then, land is sighted. As everyone rushes to the bows, Jim is able to get himself out of the barrel without being observed. How should he now warn the others? As it happens, Dr Livesey sends Jim to fetch his pipe and tobacco. In the open, in full sight (but not hearing) of everyone else on deck, Jim is able to convey to the doctor that he has something important to tell him, and please can he get the captain and the squire together in the main cabin?

I won't go on, scene by scene. The fact is that these scenes are linked, and not obviously. It's called narrative drive. There is no point where you say to yourself, "Aha! That's the hook that keeps me turning the pages," but that is exactly what it is. The story has a momentum that carries the reader onwards. At every stage we want to learn what happens next, and Jim is carried by the narrative into every fresh situation. Every scene, every chapter feeds into the next, taking the reader's attention and interest with it.

*

So, finally, you have your idea and you have your plot to express it. Who do you want the plot to happen to?

The Characters

Novels are about people – your characters. Readers enter your world through the eyes of these people, and get to know and engage with them through the meanings and the intentions of their words and actions.

Here's a couple of simplistic (BOCTAOE!) but still pretty much true rules:

- A novel should be about the most important thing that has happened to the protagonist up to that point in their life.
- The protagonist should change, preferably for the better, in the course of the novel.

Without both of those, then really there's no story.

Characters must hook the reader's interest. We want tension so that they are constantly overcoming something. Even a scene as simple as waking up in the morning needs a sense of challenge being overcome. Of narrative drive – that term again. They do not react blindly to events but initiate them. That is how we come to know them, and either root for them if they're the good guys or look forward to their comeuppance if they're the bad ones. Either way, it's how you make us interested and teach us to care what happens to them.

They must have a voice. This doesn't mean they must speak physically (though that does help). The way they speak, think and act are all distinct, so that at no point does the reader have to remind themselves who they are, or guess who is talking right now.

The main character, the hero, is the protagonist. They will have sidekicks and quite possibly an enemy (the antagonist), all of whom need at least a little sketching out; and there may be a host of supporting roles who might not need more than a couple of lines.

WHOSE STORY?

For *His Majesty's Starship,* I had the ideas for a novel but still no sense of what or who the book was *about.* How do I express all that in an adventure that people will want to read? The book didn't have an *about* until I re-read C.S. Forester's Hornblower series. I had read these books as a child but there was one aspect of them that I had never grasped, back then: Hornblower is a depressive. For all his heroism, he cannot believe he's any good. Every mission he goes on, he is convinced it will be his last, because this will be the time when he gets recognised as a fraud and gets sacked. Or shot.

And now I had my hero, the protagonist of *His Majesty's Starship*. A depressive ship's captain who was once seen as a hotshot but in fact has never risen above a certain level of command. All his contemporaries are leagues ahead of him in terms of rank and prestige… And that is exactly why he hits it off with the aliens while others don't. The other captains all command large crews; he commands a crew of six.

Now I had him, that was what the book was *about*. It's about a man who thinks he's a failure learning he's actually pretty good, in the right circumstances. And once I had him, I could bring the other ideas – the ones that kicked the book off in the first place – into play, and I could come up with a plot that allowed me to express it all.

THE NAME'SH BOND…

Let's go back to James Bond. Think of what you know about 007, whether the version of various movies or the subtly different man who appears in the books. The latter of course is the version that the world knew first. Ian Fleming could never quite decide how old Bond was: at first it's mentioned that he was doing work for the Secret Service before the war, while in later books he was still a teenager when war broke out. Not that the two are incompatible; and it's not important because when we first meet him he is already an experienced secret agent with a high body count behind him. If you called him a hedonistic mildly alcoholic tobacco addicted womanising misogynist then you would not be far off. The taste for terrible puns is only in the movies.

But did you know that Bond gets his heart broken in *Casino Royale*? For the first time in his life he is truly in love – and she turns out to be a double agent. In the very last line of the book he reports back to London and snarls that the bitch is dead.[8] We catch only a glimpse of that broken heart just before the scar tissue grows over it.

I first met the Bond of the books when I was a child and we inherited the complete set. I picked one at random and eagerly started reading. It was *You Only Live Twice*, which opens with Bond on the verge of being sacked from the Secret Service. His wife Tracy was killed at the end of the previous book, *On Her Majesty's Secret Service*, and he is suffering a complete breakdown. I found it incomprehensible. This was not the Bond of the movies that I knew.

I tried another. *Goldfinger*, which opens with a depressed Bond suffering a one-body-too-many bout of angst in Miami airport, having just had to kill a drug dealer in self defence.

You Only Live Twice ends on a cliffhanger, with an amnesiac Bond about to fall into the hands of the KGB. The following and final novel, *The Man with the Golden Gun*, opens with a brainwashed Bond trying to assassinate M.

The point being, Bond is a much more complex character than you would realise if you only knew him from the movies. Ian Fleming could have just given us a series of stories about a suave, near indestructible super spy. But they would not have been nearly half as good.

Fleming knew the rules that I've mentioned above. He knew that the Bond at the end of each book had to be different to the one at the start, and the readers had to care about the transformation. This is why so many series start to go off or become formulaic after a while: there is only so much transformation and development that one character

---

8   A line that Daniel Craig just threw away, in my opinion; though the movie did retain the book's gruesome torture scene, which is the kind of thing that never happened to Sean Connery.

can go through. It's always, "His most baffling case yet!" and never, "A doddle compared to the last one".

And what about the other characters? Really, they are up to you. The opposite of the protagonist is the antagonist: simplistically, the villain. And then there's all the others who appear as the story unfolds. There's no hard and fast rule, and certainly the rules above do not necessarily apply to every single person who appears in your book – but the more complex the cast is, by and large, the more satisfying the novel becomes. Some of these people might already be in your head. Otherwise, as the plot develops, it can create character-shaped holes that you need to fill.

For *H.M.S. Barabbas* I had a whole book full of existing characters that I could use – Jim, Dr Livesey, Long John Silver and all the rest from the original *Treasure Island*. Stevenson's novel went safely out of copyright in 1964, so I could do what I liked with them. In the end I only used Jim and Livesey. Maybe Silver will make a return appearance one day – but I thought that bringing him straight back would still be a bit too much 'Return to Treasure Island'. Meanwhile, to make the novel mine, I needed more characters of my own.

First, the antagonist. I decided that Jim would meet the (half) brother of Israel Hands, the pirate he kills in *Treasure Island*. This led to the creation ex nihilo of Captain Malachi Hands. Who else?

There's a singular dearth of female characters in *Treasure Island*: Mrs Hawkins is the only one, and her only purpose is to exist for Jim to think of her from time to time. You could get away with that in 1883; not so much nowadays, and nor should you want to.

Jim must travel through Plymouth, so he needs somewhere to stay until his ship arrives. Who else should he stay with but Dr Livesey's widowed sister? Who happens to have two Jim-aged daughters? Cue Mrs Caroline Aitken, and Lydia and Joanna.

He doesn't get to London, of course. He is press ganged and ends up on Hands' ship, H.M.S. *Barabbas*. Captains don't usually involve themselves with the affairs of the sailors before the mast; they have first officers for that. Cue Mr Bale.[9] Hands is much more sophisticated than his half brother but just as evil; Bale is just evil.

Meanwhile, as a sidekick, for this and future adventures, Jim meets the ship's boy, Richard Palmer. And if Jim isn't to learn his doctoring from an actual doctor in London, he can at least make a start on *Barabbas* itself. Cue the alcoholic but extremely competent Dr Wilequet.

And it isn't just the villains, Hands and Bale, who provide the drama. A story is always much more interesting when its characters don't get along. Dr Livesey's family strongly disapprove of Jim because they've read his bragging, first person account of how he came by his wealth; in other words, they've read *Treasure Island*. As has Hands, which is why he's so interested in having Jim on board: here is a boy who knows where there's treasure. Jim is decent and

---

9   As my own little joke, apart from Jim, Livesey and Hands, every male character is named after an actor who has played Jim on screen. Christian Bale was Jim to Charlton Heston's Silver in a 1990 film version of *Treasure Island*.

honourable – a legacy of the original novel – while Richard has lived most of his life surrounded by criminals; they are not natural allies. Dr Wilequet drinks to mask his self-loathing; Jim immediately despises him, until he comes to realise the man's proficiency as a surgeon and his reasons for doing what he does.

And what of Jim himself? I could work with his established flaws. Jim is refined by hardship, having his priggishness knocked out of him, bringing out his innate decency and emerging the better for it. He will always be a combination of innocent abroad and able to sup with the devil, but he can have self-knowledge too.

STARRING...

For all of the above, I wrote a character profile. Age; gender; height; physical appearance; distinguishing characteristics of speech and habits. Their characters, their backgrounds, the arcs of their own stories if applicable. Who they *are*. Having this written down before you start saves having to cudgel your brains to think of how to make this person distinguishable from the others, and saves the classic boob of someone changing eye or hair colour – and occasionally name or gender – between scenes.

You may find it helpful to have a cast list for your novel. I use the term advisedly because I like to base the characters – if only their appearance – on real life actors[10] that I can imagine portraying them. This is handy shorthand when it comes to writing their profile. The actor's identity does not have to be revealed to the reader – it's more fun to let them

---

10 Real-life acquaintances too, sometimes.

do their own imagining – and of course in my head I could cast a book with a dream team, both living and dead and from any stage of their careers.[11]

This, again, is a stage your ghostwriter can help with if you're finding it too much.

The Writing

Last but not least is the writing itself: the actual conveying of your ideas and plot and the characters within it, in words put down on a page.

One of the hardest things to wrap your braincells around is that, when it comes to creative writing there are no rules.

Well, there *are* rules, of course. But not in the same way that academic papers must all follow a certain style in their references, or infinitives must never be split, or you don't change viewpoints within the same paragraph (though that last one should only be violated under close supervision).

This is especially hard to grasp if you were taught anything at all about English at school, because chances are your English teacher had very strong views on what was right and what was not. But, as A.C. Hilton put it: "though they wrote it all by rote, they did not write it right."

The most important judge of your writing is the reader. If you're speaking to them then you're getting it right.

And now, with all that freedom staring you in the face, you may suddenly realise it's not as easy as it sounds.

---

11 My dream production of *H.M.S. Barabbas* includes Anthony Head as Hands, Colin Baker as Wilequet and – um – Christian Bale as Bale, all of whom are alive at the time of writing.

Says Who?

Here's an easy decision to make. Should your story be in the first or third person?

But that's not as easy as it sounds, either. Stevenson wrote *Treasure Island* as a first person narrative from the point of view of Jim (to whom this is *definitely* the most important thing to have happened in his life up to this date). The opening paragraph tells us that the other survivors of the expedition have asked him to write down 'the whole particulars' of what happened on that island. As a result we see the action through the eyes of a steadily-becoming-less-innocent boy. As Jim cowers in the apple barrel and overhears the pirates plotting to murder his friends, or as Israel Hands chases him up the rigging of *Hispaniola* with nowhere left to run, we are *there*. But Stevenson found he got bogged down. One problem with a first person narrative is that things may be happening elsewhere in the story, and if the viewpoint character isn't present, there's no way for the reader to know about it.

That is why, on the island, the story abruptly skips from Jim's first person narration to extracts from Dr Livesey's diary, then back again. The change helped Stevenson pick up the impetus and also, once he had written it down, gave him the opportunity to introduce a little non-linearity that kept the readers engaged.

Flowery Phrases

What is your voice?

The author's voice sets the tone of the whole thing. If you are setting the story in a dystopian post-industrial wasteland then you don't use the vocabulary of a sylvan pastoral idyll.

Even though it's about writing poetry, Lewis Carroll's poem 'Poeta Fit, Non Nascitur',[12] contains very helpful advice about writing in general – in particular to look at life "With a sort of mental squint".

> *"For instance, if I wished, Sir,*
> *Of mutton-pies to tell,*
> *Should I say 'dreams of fleecy flocks*
> *Pent in a wheaten cell'?"*
> *"Why, yes," the old man said: "that phrase*
> *Would answer very well."*

You don't want a voice that just says "He did this," or "She did that." You want a turn of phrase, a style, the occasional little verbal bomb that the readers come to expect and enjoy. You want to be poetic, even if you're not writing a poem. Analogies, shades of meaning, subtle ambiguities of phrase.

John Wyndham once wrote a story called 'Consider Her Ways'. He took the title from one of my favourite Bible verses, from the King James Version:

> *'Go to the ant, thou sluggard; consider her ways, and be wise!'* (Proverbs 6.6, KJV)

Here is the same verse from the deliberately more modern and accessible Good News Translation:

> *'Lazy people should learn a lesson from the way ants live.'* (GNT)

---

12 'A Poet Is Made, Not Born'.

They both say exactly the same thing, but there's a reason why Wyndham did not call his story, 'Learn A Lesson'.

Earlier I said that my novel *His Majesty's Starship* was "ground zero for all kinds of ideas swarming about in my head". I could have just said that several different ideas came together in the writing, but where's the fun in that?

You might yourself be more inclined towards the GNT than the KJV. You might favour the more modern and accessible style. But whether you want your prose plain and simple, or so purple that it kills insects (see, I did it again!) you want an evocative tone that can trigger the reader's imagination. Writing is about more than just getting the words down.

Make It Real

The world of your characters has to be as real in your head as the world around you. If you get the feeling that it's all just theatre scenery, packed away the moment you stop watching it, then you're doing it wrong. How do you make your world real?

Well, Stevenson probably hadn't met any real life pirates. What he had done was travel to America and back; so, he could write about a long sea voyage. I don't know if he based any of his characters on real life acquaintances, but there is no reason why he should not have. Ian Fleming drew heavily on his experiences of gambling and intelligence work for verisimilitude. The point where his experiences blurred into fiction is unimportant. What matters is that he made it feel real.

I've never worn a spacesuit – but I have scuba dived, so I

know what it is like to wear a slightly claustrophobic outfit that manages to give you remarkable freedom of movement, and yet could kill you with the slightest malfunction. I've never flown a spaceship or a jet fighter – but I have driven a car (and piloted a glider solo) so I know what it's like to be in charge of a powerful machine, making its movements an extension of my own body. I've never time travelled to a medieval city – but I have been in some pretty insalubrious present day third world metropoles, so if I want to imagine a city with no underground sewers or modern amenities, that is where my imagination goes. We have five senses, of which the most powerful and oft forgotten is smell, so an author uses them all.

The Big Picture

And then there is the whole structure of the story. Themes and ideas run through it from beginning to end, like connecting fibres.

In a detective story, the clue cannot just emerge as something the detective saw but no one else did; the reader has to have been shown it too, without realising its significance.

There's a dramatic principle called Chekov's Pistol, written down by Anton Chekhov: if a gun appears in a story then at some point or other it should be fired.[13] The reader can have fun working out how and when and why it will be fired; even better, after it is fired, they may be impressed by

---

13 Amor Towles' *A Gentleman in Moscow* pays marvellous tribute to Chekov by taking this quite literally; there is some thirty years of narrative between the pistol's first appearance, and its use.

your brilliance in not even drawing attention to the gun on its first appearance, though now they realise, it's obvious.

And if the protagonist is changed – as they should be – by the end of the book, then the change can't just happen in the last chapter. It has to be gradual throughout the story.

I think the most valuable lesson I ever learned in novel writing was from my time with Working Partners, and that is the chapter outline. Until then I wrote my novels by working through the plot as I saw it, changing scene and point of view when it seemed appropriate, generally pantsing the whole thing. My editor, Amber Caraveo, insisted on a chapter outline, and she was right. With a chapter outline you know where you are, and where you ought to be, and where you're heading. Every day, when you sit down to write, you know what you will be writing. When it comes to themes, you can follow them through the plot at a glance. Thanks, Amber!

Of course, like any plan of action, the chapter outline might not survive contact with the enemy. As you write, you might see that scenes work better knocked together, or pushed apart, or switched around. But you have the outline. Use it.

Summing Up

Remember the lady I mentioned in the Introduction? By now I hope it's clear why I couldn't just write her two chapters without knowing a whole lot more beside. I didn't know the characters; I didn't know what was happening; I didn't know at what stage in her life we were meant to be.

If I was starting her life from scratch then I didn't know where we were going; if I was writing at a later stage in her life then I didn't know how we had got there.

If you want to hire a ghostwriter then everything in this chapter is something that will need working out. Don't feel daunted, because it is all doable. Your ghost is there to help you out.

3. What Goes Into Publishing A Novel?

One more section before deciding whether you need to hire a ghostwriter, because you need to understand this bit too.

You pay your ghostwriter off and send your carefully honed manuscript to a publisher. An offer arrives. You sign the contract, sit back, and a few months later your book is published. Right?

Well…

I said earlier that there are many cogs in the mechanism that gets your book published. Here are some more.

It might turn out you need your ghostwriter to come back.

Enter the Editors

In Appendix 1, 'What Do I Do With My Manuscript?' I look at the available options for when you have your manuscript written: finding a traditional publisher, or self-publishing. If you find a traditional publisher then all of what follows, apart from the actual writing, should be done in-house and at their expense. If you decide to self-publish, then you will need to pay for all this and full disclosure makes me say that a ghostwriter probably won't be your only expense.

BUT CAN'T THE GHOSTWRITER ALSO...

No, they can't.

Let me rephrase that.

The ghostwriter will turn in the best manuscript they can. They will check it for spelling, sense and everything else to within an inch of its life. That goes without saying.

But they are the worst people for spotting any extra work that needs doing, simply because they are too close to it. They will be able to stare unblinking at a paragraph containing an absolutely glaring error, and not see it, because in their mind's eye they see it only as it should be. They will miss the fact that the culprit could not possibly have left footprints across the back lawn as we have already established they came in through the front door, because they wrote both versions and so both are equally true in their heads. They will be unable to see that Chapter 7 could be cut by 50% because that is the chapter they spent the most time on and they are *so proud* of it.

A book needs editors who are not the writer.

Someone else needs to do all of what follows – though I will concede there is a lot of BOCTAOE in what you're about to read.

It's Not Just the Words

For the rest of this chapter I will assume you have gone the traditional publishing route.

First of all, it is very unlikely your book will just appear as is.

Assuming a commissioning editor can't find any reason not to refuse it without finishing the manuscript first, they will read it through from beginning to end. That's when they decide they can convince their sales team that they are onto a winner, and will therefore make you an offer commensurate with what they think they will get back from the publication. (If they can't convince the sales team then forget it. This is why the classic rejection letter is a variation on "Does not fit into our list at this time.")

The book moves slightly further down the conveyor belt towards publication…

Next, it will be read again, with nitpicking in mind. It will receive a structural edit. An extra set of eyes, not previously acquainted with the work, will go through it scene by scene. At this stage, their main concern is with the flow of the writing. Simplistically (BOCTAOE) a story should follow a three-act structure:

- Act 1, everything is going swimmingly for the hero;
- Act 2, everything goes horribly wrong;
- Act 3, everything is put right and better than before.

To achieve this, are there any scenes where you get bogged down; are there any scenes that could be extended; are the scenes in the right order; does the action step up in the right places? Is there anything that could be added, or – gasp – cut?

Then there's developmental editing. Do the themes develop in the right way? Are the characters consistent?

Of course, the publishers aren't going to make these changes themselves. It's your book. Once the book has gone through all this, the manuscript will come back to you, with their suggestions.

Alternatively, the commissioning editor might pre-empt some of these stages by making suggestions which, *if you respond to them in the right way*, will lead to an offer being made.[14] If you already have an offer then the suggestions might be more negotiable – but either way, bear in mind that they're publishing it on their penny and you would like them to believe in it, wouldn't you?

So, it's just possible that your ghostwriter has more work to do.

Rewriting the Rewrites

Having my first novel picked up by Scholastic began the first of quite a few rewrites. It had come under the gaze of David Fickling – the man who published Philip Pullman, so let's just say I could assume he knew what he was doing. Prior to our first meeting, my agent warned me that David felt the novel was too bogged down in detail. I went to the meeting forewarned of this and determined to prove him wrong. I came away convinced of his point of view.[15]

So: a new opening chapter, throwing us straight into the action. A space battle, a few people killed. All good stuff. I sent off the rewrite.

---

14 David Fickling at Scholastic made it very clear that if he felt I was only going through the motions of responding to his suggested rewrites of *His Majesty's Starship*, without my heart being in it, then the offer was off the table.

15 My first card on the table was insisting that the alien sex scene stayed. "Absolutely," he said cheerfully. He says a lot of things cheerfully, including carefully enumerating your novel's precise faults.

And he didn't like it. I began to see the problem: I had added more plot, but left the excess verbiage in as well. David did me a huge favour for life at this point by recommending that I read Patrick O'Brian's *Master & Commander*, first of the Aubrey series. O'Brian's characters just slide into the action. By the end of page 1 the two main characters, Aubrey and Maturin, have met; by the end of page 2 they have taken a hearty dislike to each other.

I decided to apply this to the novel and I cut out anything that didn't directly relate to the action, including (though it broke my heart) the chapter in which the alien Arm Wild interviews the crew of the eponymous starship. I was so proud of that chapter: it was key to introducing not only the crew but also the alien mindset to the reader. The novel was now down to 92,000 words, from its first draft of 113,000.

Back to Scholastic, and David courted death with a casual comment along the lines of: "Don't I remember a chapter where Arm Wild interviews the crew? I quite miss that…"

I restrained my homicidal impulse and learnt the lesson: anything that develops the characters is probably acceptable, even if it doesn't contribute to the action. The interview was reinstated.

Now It's the Words

So, I finally had a workable text which was tighter, punchier and infinitely better than the first version David read. In fact I should say now that I have never had an editorial encounter, with any book, that has not made the book much better.

Then came the fun of the copy edit.

The copy editor does more than just check the spelling (that's the proof reader's job, anyway). They have to check house style and tone. David wanted to develop an imprint punchier than the usual Scholastic children's material, which is why he took this book, but not everyone at Scholastic had got this memo. At one point a character is forced into a difficult decision; as he commits to one course of action, he mutters, "Sod it."

People do not say, "Sod it" in Scholastic books. This was frowningly changed to, "Damn it."

We compromised on, "Nuts."

The eponymous starship of the novel, being a space vessel, has attitude thrusters – small rockets that control its roll and pitch and yaw (in other words, in the word's technical sense, attitude), given that in the vacuum of space it can't use control planes and rudders like an aircraft would.

The copy editor helpfully changed every mention of these items to 'altitude thrusters' – a term that is meaningless in space. I changed every mention back.

Fortunately, the copy edit is much more negotiable than the other stages. You might have good reasons for wanting particular words to appear in that way. But it is a stage that will need your attention.

Selling the Thing

Above all else, your publisher's marketing department

needs to sell your book. It needs publicity; it needs bookshops to pick it up. And the prime mover of this process will be... you. You know the book better than anyone else. You can wax lyrical on its strengths. You can tell them what it's about. It all begins with you. This was already true when my first novel was published in 1998 and it is ten times so now; marketing departments have been slashed to make ends meet, and social media has gone from nothing to almost everything. Someone has to do the selling, and that person is probably you. Or your ghostwriter. Or both of you, working together.

And so, we come to the big question...

4. Should I Hire A Ghostwriter?

By now you should have a pretty good idea of what is required in writing a novel – by which I mean, all the things to take care of, alongside the sheer ability to write in the first place. You know what will be required of you, and what the ghostwriter can do, and – perhaps even more important – what *else* the ghostwriter can do.

With all that in mind, I hope you can make an informed decision, and that the decision is 'Yes'.

But first, there is one other attractive-looking option that has crept its way into the public discourse in recent years, and for all I know it's hovering before your eyes at this very moment. So, let me knock it on the head, right here, right now.

Can't I Just Use AI?

Think how far technology has developed in recent years so that we can even think of asking this question. A decade ago, five years even, this would have been unthinkable as a serious question in the real world, though as usual science fiction got there way ahead of you. In Isaac Asimov's short story 'Galley Slave' (published in 1957), a disgruntled academic sues the company that supplied the robot used to proofread his book, claiming it made changes behind his back that made him look stupid.[16] In recent news as I write, an American lawyer got into trouble for using ChatGPT to conduct his legal research. Ever eager to please, it invented some completely imaginary cases to cite as references. Asimov's concerns about the accuracy of AI-generated text were really quite prescient.

In *Nineteen Eighty-Four* (published in 1949), Winston Smith's girlfriend Julia has "some mechanical job on one of the novel-writing machines". The Party churns out a whole slew of literature, music, drama and entertainment designed to keep the masses happy, including "sentimental songs which were composed entirely by mechanical means on a special kind of kaleidoscope known as a versificator."

The idea of machines creating art is not new, though it took Orwell to give it the wonderfully sneering label, 'prolefeed'.[17]

So, of course you can use AI. It will be much cheaper and a lot quicker than hiring a human. It will also produce disposable pap, but if that's what you want then go for it. Money for nothing. And it's happening. A good friend recently lost a major income stream as the website she was providing content for decided to use ChatGPT instead. It makes no difference to the website's owners that the product is flat, insincere, dry and devoid of any human feeling.[18] What matters to them is that it's cheap.

---

16 You have to ask why he didn't read the proofs before committing to print. Perhaps he was not the brightest academic to begin with. Elsewhere, I will tell the sad but hilarious story of an author who didn't check what their ghostwriter had provided.

17 You can take the boy out of Eton but you can't take Eton out of the boy. Even if the boy is George Orwell.

18 Rather, it does of course make a difference – but not the one they were hoping for.

Nor is it just the bean counters who are turning to AI. In 2023 Neil Clarke, editor of the online science fiction magazine *Clarkesworld*, wrote that there had been a surge of AI-generated submissions to the magazine by authors desperate to get into print but not prepared to do anything so old fashioned as get good at writing first.

But I will assume you have a measure of pride and would like to put some effort into your book. Besides, why should anyone want to read something no one could be bothered to write? (I wish I could claim the credit for that thought but I can't; I forget where on social media I heard it but it is worth repeating.)

WHAT IS IT GOOD FOR?

In the interests of fairness, I will concede AI has some uses. Sometimes all the human imagination needs is a nudge, and AI can provide that. Many authors already use little devices to get the wheels turning in their minds: story prompt cards which you can draw from a pack, or throwing dice, or the I Ching. AI is no different to that. Perhaps, if I had been stuck for a way to get Jim Hawkins on board H.M.S. *Barabbas*, I could have asked ChatGPT and it could have suggested the press gang, as one of a list of options. It would then have been up to me, the human, to research how the press gang worked to make that scene and its developments realistic.[19]

But, neither ChatGPT nor any other AI can manage

---

19 I did *not* use AI. I was inspired by an essay called 'A Pressed Man', by Robert Hay, published in 1811 and included in *The Mammoth Book of Life Before the Mast*, ed. Jon E. Lewis, published by Robinson, 2001.

original inspiration, for a very good reason. They do not create anything. They are trained by studying hundreds and thousands of examples of the kind of thing they are being asked to produce, and then told to do likewise.[20] Science fiction has given us the idea that an AI is an intellect vast and cool and unsympathetic that can plunder massive datasets to produce absolutely accurate information at the drop of an electron. Only the bit about plundering massive datasets is correct. In fact it is all about probability. ChatGPT and its ilk string together words and themes and ideas based on what *probably* comes next, according to the information they have studied so far. The result is a bit like listening to a speech by Boris Johnson. It all sounds plausible, until you realise that even he has no idea what word ought to come next and he picks the one that sounds about right.

When fantasy author Juliet E. McKenna was starting her career in the early 1990s, she was told by an editor that her manuscript was a perfectly competent fantasy novel, "but there's nothing to distinguish this from the six other perfectly competent fantasy novels that land on my desk every week". It was then left up to her purely human, imaginative, creative mind to make it different, which she did. Cue a successful, award-winning career, now in its third decade.

So, AI can copy, yes. It can pastiche, and it can do it very well. But, it cannot originate. In contrast, most works of any kind of art are sparked in the creator's mind by thinking, "What if…?" They then pursue the idea, often developing

---

20 The ethics of this are another matter and beyond the remit of this book, but you could do a lot worse than read the statement by the Society of Authors in the 'Further Reading' section.

as they go. I've described how *His Majesty's Starship* was the result of a "What it?" thought about a Royal Space Force, plus several ideas coming in from all over the field of science fiction: some of which inspired me, some of which I wanted to deliver my own take on, some of which actively irritated me and needed putting right.

Stories so often come from an idea an author wants to explore, or improve on; and on top of that, they then add their own take on ethics, values, feelings… The things that can never be listed on a spreadsheet or reduced to bytes in a dataset, but which are the residue of our entire human experience.

LET'S HEAR IT FOR ENTROPY

By now in this book, I hope you have a feel for what else a ghostwriter can do for you. You can work together to tease out stories and ideas, and work collaboratively with them to produce something that's more than the sum of its parts.

AI can never make something that is more. Only less. It just copies – and any copy is always inferior to the original.[21]

So, while AI continues to learn from human-created examples, it will at best produce perfectly competent work with nothing to distinguish it from any other perfectly competent work. Eliminate human input and it will only be able to learn off poorer and poorer AI-generated examples, spiralling ever further down into bland mediocre sludge that makes Orwell's prolefeed look highbrow. To many outlets requiring text, like the website my friend worked

---

21   We have the Second Law of Thermodynamics to blame for that.

for, that won't matter. To anyone requiring something new and different – otherwise known as thinking readers and, I hope, including you – it will.

Go with the human.

5. Finding And Hiring That Ghost

Ghostwriters are very easy to find. Just Google 'finding a ghostwriter'.

Finding the right one, though…

The Google search I just mentioned will take you to sites like Upwork, Reedsy, Fiverr and Freelancer.com. I have my own opinions about these sites which I have no intention of sharing here, because actually in a couple of cases they do have a good reputation, they look out for their members and you could do a lot worse – but if I said which ones then the others might complain.

You will also find agencies and collectives of ghostwriters, and I suggest starting your search there. Quite apart from anything else, agencies are more selective about who they take onto their books in the first place – so, the mere fact of a ghost belonging is a good sign. I immediately think of entities like United Ghostwriters (**https://www. unitedghostwriters.co.uk/**) and The Ghostwriters Agency (**https://www.theghostwritersagency.com/**), because – full disclosure – I'm a member of both.

Depending on how well the agency represents itself to the world then it's over to you to do some research.

How Do I Know They're Any Good?

There is one obvious drawback when it comes to finding a ghostwriter. Normally, when you're looking for someone to do a job then you want to know what else they've done; and in most other jobs, they can tell you. Ghostwriters are often contractually barred from doing so.

A ghost can at least get a reference from a publisher; Client Zero's editors can confirm I've done work for them, without saying on whose behalf it was. And there may be acknowledgements in printed books that the ghost can proudly wave under your nose.

In my case, I can (and will) point at the corpus of work in my own name, and I find that to be pretty persuasive. I won't deny I have also been known to wave a copy of my ghosted work at the webcam during a Zoom meeting with a prospective client; the client is informed, they get the hint, and the author's name has never passed my lips.

Chemistry

A really successful collaboration ultimately depends on the chemistry between ghost and author. So, once you have your likely suspects lined up, make contact. Have a chat on Zoom. Describe your project, and see what comes back at you. If this is the right ghost for you then they will start engaging straight off. They will be saying things that show they get it. They might even be challenging you, pointing out things that hadn't occurred to you. And, hopefully, you will find the experience reassuring. You will feel you're in the hands of a pro.

In 'How Fiction Works' I talked about having a chapter outline and character profiles. Perhaps you could first of all hire the ghost to develop these for you. It will be a smaller outlay if you treat it as a separate job, and you can use their work to help you make the final decision. The exercise will also help them become more engaged in the project, so that when you've decided they are the one you want to write your novel, they will already have large chunks of it in their head.

And remember that any interview works both ways: both parties are interviewing one another. The one who pays the piper calls the tune – but it is the piper who knows more about matters such as rhythm, tempo, key, the appropriate music for the occasion, and so on. If the payer has any sense, they will consult and respect that expertise. In the end, both parties need to be sure they're going to work well with each other beforehand.

FOR GHOSTWRITERS

6. Someone Wants To Hire Me!

Congratulations! You have obviously made your mark. To have someone want you for your writing is a huge compliment.

Some publishers don't use the term 'ghostwriter'. They prefer 'co-author'. I'm not sure whether this is meant to be a sop to anyone's ego, so say it loud and proud: "I am a ghostwriter!"

This isn't the place to tell you how to write fiction in the first place. If you've got to the stage where someone might want to hire you, we can assume you've already overcome several hurdles.[22] You know how to structure a story. You can bash out chapter and character outlines without breaking a sweat. You've mastered the splinter of ice that Graham Greene said lurks in every author's heart.

I assume this opportunity has fallen into your lap from one of two sources. You could have been approached by a publisher or an agent; or, this could be a purely private

---

22 But if you really need advice then, okay, there are many how-to guides out there. Stephen King's *On Writing* immediately comes to mind. More recently there is Gareth L. Powell's *About Writing: A Field Guide for Aspiring Authors*. If, like me, you want to start in science fiction then I can recommend Orson Scott Card's *How to Write Science Fiction and Fantasy*.

arrangement between you and an individual. Some of what follows is more applicable to one than the other; some is equally applicable to both. (I go into the legal and financial sides of ghostwriting in separate chapters.)

What Does The Author Want?

As a fiction writer you are aware of the structure of text. You know it's not just about stringing words together into sentences. It's about making them flow.

Not every author will know this, however. They may have their own ideas. One author decided no chapter should be more than 1,000 words and so (after I had delivered the final draft, so was no longer involved) slashed the chapters ruthlessly, even in the middle of dialogue and even if he was cutting information that would be needed for later. When he finally got around to telling me of this requirement, I had just finished the first draft of the latest book. He asked me to "take twenty minutes" to make sure no chapter was over the magic limit. It took more than that…

So, get to know your author. If they are a big name and the contact has come through their agents or publishers then this might not be as easy as it sounds, but at the very least, read what else they have written (or has come out in their name), and find out the intended ethos and purpose of the book. A plot outline alone is not enough, though they might think it is. It's their name going on the cover and you need to know exactly who they are. This might not have occurred to them, because they already know themselves so well that they don't see how other people could not.

Establish Expectations

For me, one of the greatest delights of being a writer is that I get to write, and I get paid for it, and once I've sent the manuscript off, someone else has to take care of the tedium of marketing and selling it. Your author, on the other hand, might not quite realise just what is entailed, or assume vaguely that because they've hired you to write, that covers all the other little details too. So, you need to establish your author's level of awareness. Someone needs to take the marketing and selling stage just as seriously as the writing stage; they need to know this and they need to know that person isn't you.[23]

Get To Know The Publishers

You have probably dealt with publishers far more often than the author has. You know the language and what to expect. You know what is a reasonable ask and what is not. Even if your sole contact has been with the author or their representative, seek out whoever will be the editor at the publisher's end and make their acquaintance. Life will be so much easier if you can talk directly to each other.

Somewhere on my hard disk is a folder with a lot of photos of one author's knees. That is because he liked to print out his manuscripts, mark them up manually, photograph them page by page (on his lap, hence the knees) and email me the pictures. This worked fine for nine out of ten photos, as long as I squinted at the writing and paid as little attention

---

23   Unless you're offering. And charging accordingly.

to the knees as I could, but inevitably something would get blurred or smudged and then I would have to phone up and seek clarification, which missed the whole point of the emailed photos. Eventually I was able to introduce him to the concept of marking text up electronically, and I'm told the publishers are forever grateful to me for doing so.

Get To Know The Material

… Ideally before any agreement is made. I was approached by an author whose novel needed to be rounded off with around five thousand words by a particular date, when it was due to be sent to a publisher for consideration. This had been previously arranged between them. From his description of the story, it was right up my street; also, I was between jobs and needed something. I said yes; everything was agreed in writing and I sent off an invoice for the first instalment of payment.

Then, fortunately, before any money had changed hands, he sent me what he had so far – and I knew within a couple of pages that he would be wasting his time if he paid me to do anything. No publisher would take this, with or without that last five thousand words. Which they would never see, because they would stop reading even sooner than I had. Nice idea, some nice bits of writing, but *a lot* of polishing needed. In short, it was just too first draft.

I was torn. On the one hand we had an agreement. On the other, I hadn't been paid yet… So, write the five thousand words and pocket the money? (Just reading what he sent took up billable time.) Or tell him it really was not worth it, to save his money and to practice being a writer himself?

The first course would probably have been justified within the field of business ethics. But I chose the second. I waived the invoice, putting it all down to experience, and the fact that I had a handy anecdote to add to this book.

7. What Makes A Good Ghostwriter?

Back in 2009, the world of science fiction was, if not rocked, then mildly titillated by an online meltdown from an author who had had a serious falling out with her ghostwriter. To be fair on her, he was a scam artist stringing her along; to be fair on him (as little as he deserves it), she really should have checked his work before publishing it. In short, he added an entire first chapter to her book which he copied direct from a novel by David Gemmell, only pausing to change the names. Quite apart from anything else, the stolen chapter had absolutely nothing to do with the rest of the book, even with the names changed. This did not stop her rushing into print.

Ghostwriters: don't be like him.[24]

Ghostwriters are entirely unregulated. There is no official accreditation, no governing body that regulates our behaviour and to which disgruntled authors can appeal. Any code of ethics exists only in our own heads. So it's up to us to set a good example for our profession.

A ghostwriter is a professional (which is one more reason you should expect to be paid properly: see 'The Money' below). Act like one.

I'd like to think that the few hints in this section already come naturally to you, but they might need saying anyway. So, without further ado...

---

24 And authors: don't be like her.

Ditch the Ego

This shouldn't need saying because you're already in the wrong job if you're after fame and glory. The degree of credit you will get is somewhere on a spectrum between full openness (like Sir Chris Hoy, mentioned earlier) and complete denial, and it will more likely tend towards the latter.

Think of all the sweat and tears you've put into developing your own voice as a writer. And now – sorry – forget it. You are now a mouthpiece for the author. You have to copy their voice and their style, and the join has to be seamless.[25] You've worked hard at becoming good enough at your job that someone will consider you as a ghostwriter in the first place, and now that must all be quietly forgotten.

But then, if you're used to writing fiction, you're already used to characters speaking in their own voices (aren't you…)? In your head, you can turn your author into another character. Their voice, their outlook, their mannerisms start to shine through, even as they develop characters of their own.

Still, there's no harm in maybe asking for a mention in the acknowledgements. Properly phrased, it will leave no doubt to those who know what your role was in bringing the book to fruition – and that is your reference for future jobs.

There will be times when you and the author have

---

25 A common reaction when people hear I'm a ghostwriter is, "Doesn't it feel odd to see your work come out under someone else's name?" I would love to know if my clients get asked the same question from the other direction: "Doesn't it feel odd to see someone else's work come out under your name?"

differing ideas on where the story should go or which way the words should flow – and unless they're actively committing libel then it's their version that wins.

As we will see in the chapter 'The Legal Side', once your work belongs to the author, they can do what they like with it. I can write beautiful, glowing, flowing prose which is then butchered by a tin-eared author in such a way that I could weep, and I have no recourse.[26] It comes with the territory.

If the end product is just too painful to behold then maybe don't push for that acknowledgement after all...

Deadlines Should Not Whoosh

You will have deadlines set. Keep to them.

My usually very high regard for the late, great Douglas Adams always takes a slight knock when I consider one of his oft-quoted quips: "I love deadlines. I love the whooshing noise they make as they go by." Throughout his life, Adams was notorious for his late delivery. You can get away with that – probably – if you're a millionaire bestselling author and you know, deep down, that it doesn't really matter how late you are because they'll still publish you when you eventually turn your manuscript in. But publishing business plans revolve around publishing books. Your delay ends up as a massive piece of grit in the smoothly turning wheels, with knock-on effects all the way down the line. Ultimately you could be affecting whether members of

---

26   Not a hypothetical example.

staff stay employed and even whether the company stays in business.

(I know, hark at me, the hack writer criticising a bestselling author whose advances on a single title probably outstrip my entire earnings to date. But it is a principle, and it applies. Adams always – eventually – laid the golden egg and so his quirks were tolerated. Most authors are not in this category. Let's assume you're one of them.)

Here's another trade secret: when a project is late coming in, the publisher doesn't go into suspended animation waiting for it to arrive. They simply move the next project on the list up one notch. Your project gets bumped, and if you're the one who missed the deadline then you are the one who bumped it.

You might even have been hired in the first place because the author doesn't entirely get deadlines themselves. Or is feeling blocked, unable to meet them for any reason. So, missing deadlines is not a luxury you can afford yourself.

Of course, any publisher will take wiggle room into account when they set the deadlines in the first place. And there will always be emergencies and upsets that interrupt the smooth flow of words. But I have worked in publishing, and I know that authors fall on a spectrum: those who turn in their manuscripts on (or even before) time at one end, and those who regard the deadline as a reminder to think about starting writing at the other. Guess which kind is more popular in the publisher's offices? Guess which kind they look forward to working with more? The publisher might not have any choice about keeping the author on, but they will have a choice about whether to keep you.

If you have a deadline in X days time, and Y words to

write before then, then it's very easy to work out the average number of words you need to be getting down every day between now and then. It's Y divided by X. You could even put it in a spreadsheet. In fact, I found very early on that a spreadsheet is your friend. You can tell at a glance where you are, where you ought to be and how far you have to go.[27]

And if you're a consistently late writer – well, you won't be a writer for much longer. The system regulates itself. And they might even hire a ghost to replace you.

Confidentiality

Learn to keep secrets. Remember that the author might unburden themselves of all kinds of stuff to you. Stuff that doesn't go into the book; and even if it did, you still shouldn't talk about it, because it shouldn't be possible for any reader to pick up the book and work out which bits really did happen and which have only been made up.

Keep that confidentiality. In 'The Legal Side' I talk about non-disclosure agreements, but – spoiler alert – they're not as effective as many people think, and even if you haven't signed one, so what? You're a professional, and professionals don't tattle.

---

27 You can even get it to draw graphs of required versus actual words per day; how far ahead or behind you are; and all kinds of other things. But that might just be me.

Series and Parallel

You might – lucky thing – find you're getting more than one client, and you need to work for them in parallel rather than series. There's nothing wrong with that; the only logical limit on what you can do is the number of hours in the day.

But it's up to you to see that your work for Client A doesn't interfere with your work for Client B. Plan your time accordingly. Like barristers, it's easiest to work on the cab rank rule – you take the clients in the order that they come (though, unlike barristers, there is no legally enforceable ethical code of conduct). If you're working for Client A and Client B comes along and you don't have capacity to work for them both at the same time and Client B offers more money – well, you *could* if you want bump Client A to the back of the queue. But I wouldn't recommend it. You'll be in breach of contract (you *do* have a contract, don't you? See 'The Legal Side') and, worse, you'll be someone whose word can't be trusted. Client B will just have to join the queue: you tell them that you can't take on any more work for [insert length of time here, which you can possibly work out from that spreadsheet, or just by looking at your well-organised calendar].

One prospective Client B came back to say they couldn't wait that long, and, "Perhaps it would help if we spoke and I described the project…" My answer was – and could only be – that I was happy to speak, and to listen, but it wouldn't make the slightest difference to my existing workload. He never came back.

And if Client B keeps trying to throw money at you,

ask them if they'd be happy to be bumped in favour of an even-better-paying Client C? Probably not. Clients value integrity.

What Else Have You Got?

A ghostwriter does not just write – or at least, this one doesn't. In the great Venn diagram of life, the circle of ghostwriting overlaps a number of other circles, all of which are in the general writing / editing / narrative area. After thirty years in publishing and communications, give or take and on and off, I can do other things too. I listed them back in the section 'What Exactly Is A Ghostwriter?'

I will assume you've accrued your own set of skills in your career. Can you work them into a ghostwriting pitch? Is there anything else you can offer a client? The broader the range of services you can offer, the more work you're likely to get.

8. Red Flags

Clients to Avoid

So far I've used my experiences with several clients, or prospective clients, to illustrate a point. I may have made mistakes with some of them, but none of them in principle would be clients to avoid. The problem was in the handling.

Other clients, however...

If you have half a morning free and want to read about the ghostwriting client from Hell, look no further than Andrew O'Hagan's account of ghosting for Julian Assange (see 'Further Reading'). Throughout, Mr O'Hagan was never less than 100% professional about the whole ghastly business. Julian Assange... had other things on his mind. It's a story of shifting expectations in who wanted what from whom and by when.

Client and ghost both need to know that the other is fully engaged in the process. I hope that by now in the book, I've shown what will be expected of both of you. If at any point you are suspecting that the other person isn't getting it, or doesn't know what they really want, that might be the point to withdraw politely and suggest they could get better representation elsewhere.

I have been the emergency ghostwriter for an author whose first choice was essentially trying to take over the book. They had it in their head that it would make an excellent film property, and were trying to shape the manuscript and narrative with that in mind. It was a historical novel, and they wanted bits that would make great cinema but were quite simply historically untrue. For some historical novels that may be par for the course, but in this case it would have destroyed the author's reputation if that version ever got published. In the end the first ghost had to be dismissed.

No author or ghost, however nightmarish, is worth breaking a contract for – but the contract can include handy break points, at which both parties can go their separate ways if needed. With all obligations up to that point met and monies owed duly paid, of course.

Boundaries to Set

Both parties need to set barriers. Those barriers are going to get quite porous during the writing process, but there must come a point where they can't be crossed. Neither party has a right to tell the other how to do their job.

Julian Assange wanted Andrew O'Hagan to write only on a stand-alone laptop with no internet access, to avoid it being tapped by the CIA. That might be a legitimate security concern, but other demands of his I would describe as less reasonable.

One author wanted me to watch a particular DVD for background to the story, and told me not to start writing until I'd seen it. I'll start writing when I feel ready to start writing, thank you; I knew there was plenty of story I could tell while I was waiting for the DVD to arrive, which I duly did.

If an author hires me to write their book, then as long as I deliver the agreed product by the agreed time, how and when I write are up to me. Not them.

FOR EVERYONE

9. The Money

"I've had a great idea. You write it and we'll split the profits."

We'll come back to that.

For the Ghostwritten:
Some Harsh Facts About Money

Here is something private clients – and perhaps too many publishers also – tend to forget.

If you're writing for yourself, then you do it in your spare time. Probably at evenings, or weekends. It doesn't earn you anything until, and if, you sell it. Meanwhile your bills, mortgage and other expenses are covered by whatever you already do to earn money. The day job. You might just treat the writing as a hobby, and that's fair enough. It's your choice.

And from this, people get the notion in their heads that you don't need to pay someone much to write.

In fact, if you're going to hire someone to sit in front of a computer all day, you really need to pay them something that at least approximates what they would get in any other job that involved sitting in front of a computer all day. Writers also have bills, mortgages and other expenses, and they can't live on air. For many years I was doing my freelance writing on the side of my day job. The contract that let me go full time freelance was for 4 × 40,000 word YA novels, and it paid in one year very nearly what I was getting for the same period as Communications Executive for a reasonably well-heeled technology company.

If you're self-employed – and most ghosts probably are – then you are effectively running a business, even if you're not actually trading as a limited company.[28] Your relationship with your client is a business relationship. You are not a charity.

Most people do understand that a ghost needs to be paid more than just peanuts, and so they settle on the statement in the first line of this chapter – or some variant thereon – as what seems like the ideal solution. That was where the lady in the Introduction was coming from, if you remember. So let's look at the idea more closely.

Some Inconvenient Truths

Here are some harsh facts about commercial publishing laid out by Elle Griffin of Elysian Press, in a blog post (see 'Further Reading') that analyses the US government's 2022 antitrust proceedings against publisher Penguin Random House, which wanted to buy publisher Simon & Schuster.

- In 2020, only 268 of all titles published sold more than 100,000 copies.
- 96% of books published that year sold fewer than 1,000 copies.

---

28 Which is something worth considering; talk to a proper accountant.

The data is American, but still applies over here. The proportions will not be hugely different. So, assume that an author's book retails for £15 and the author gets a 12% royalty on sales. That's £1.80 per sale. If you have a 100,000 copy bestseller then, congratulations, that's £180,000. Certainly worth splitting 50-50 with your ghost.

If, as is more likely, your book sells around the 1,000 copy mark…

£1,800.

Nine hundred quid each.

And you will probably sell fewer than that.

Nine hundred pounds is still better than a slap in the face with a wet fish. But – a quick Google search tells me – at the time of writing, the national minimum wage in the UK for someone aged over 21 working 35 hours per week is £20,820, and the average salary for an office worker is £26,347. So, nine hundred pounds is less than two weeks' work.

I am prepared to bet that your book takes a lot longer than two weeks to write.

DISCOUNTS AND HEAVY DISCOUNTS

It gets worse. The scenario above is from an ideal world where the Net Book Agreement is still in force (look it up) and booksellers buy their stock at sensible discounts from wholesalers. A typical wholesale discount will be around 35%. The bookshop then sells the title to the customer at cover price, and pockets the difference.

But this is where the hidden forces of heavily discounted

sales kick in. Chances are good that most of your sales today won't be through a bookshop; they will be through outlets like Amazon and supermarkets, which demand far higher discounts – 50% or more. And your contract will almost certainly include a clause that royalties on heavily discounted copies are based on the actual sale price, not the cover price. Your 12% royalty is no longer even 12% of the £15 cover price but probably a lower percentage of the net price received for the sale.[29]

My colleague Ian Shircore has blogged about this in more detail: see the 'Further Reading' section for the link. The takeaway point of his blog is that in the second half of 2023 his title *Conspiracy* had 18,000 new sales... generating royalties of £1,832. His book can reasonably count as a bestseller, with lifetime sales of 60,000 copies since 2022. But as he notes, "I'd have to write four or five of these a year, every year, to make even a modest income." And those sales were only made possible because of that heavy discounting.

ADVANCE AND BE RECOGNISED

The one ray of light here is the advance you will probably get if you have a professional publisher. Money up front, in the form of a non-returnable loan against royalties. You won't receive any royalties until the advance is earned out,

---

29 Which is why I don't buy books at supermarkets and will only use Amazon (for books that Amazon doesn't actually publish) as a last resort or in emergencies. If you want to buy books online in a way that benefits the author, either buy direct from the publisher's own site, or – best of all, if you're in the UK – place your order through Bookshop.org, which benefits your local bookshop too.

i.e. the book has generated enough royalties to cover the advance in the first place; but if that never happens, you get to pocket the difference and don't have to repay the unearned portion.

Say your book is so good that the publisher gives an unusually high advance for a debut author – say, £5,000. That's a lot more than the royalty-based sums we've been talking about so far. A 50-50 split means £2,500 for the ghost, so…

A month and a half's pay at minimum wage.

How long did the book take to write, again?

The book's best sales will be in its first year. Say it sells 1,000 copies through actual bookshops. Your royalty cut, £1,800, still isn't enough to pay off your two grand advance. So, you don't see any of it in Year 1.

In Year 2 and onwards, sales are down to a trickle, and they stay that way until the publishers finally put the book out of its misery and make it out of print.

In the end, you never repay the advance, and that £2,500 split is all either author or ghost ever get.

AN ESPECIALLY OBVIOUS EXCEPTION

You might have self-published, of course. See Appendix 1, 'What Do I Do With My Manuscript?' for more on that option. There's no advance, no money up front – but you get to keep every penny of profit, way above a 12% royalty per sale. It's looking rosier.

But it will be up to you to reach even those 1,000 sales. It will be a lot of work and effort. Everything else I just said still applies.

Where Does It All Come From?

So, how exactly do publishers make their money? Three ways:

1. Selling on of rights. They will pay you for the right to publish your book in English, and then sell the right to publishers in other countries to translate it and publish it there. (The author should get a cut of these sales too.) Dramatisations for TV, film, radio or stage are another possibility.
2. The long tail. Even if the publisher has a list of books that only sell a handful of copies, year on year, the fact is they *are* selling, and creating a trickle of income. All those trickles add up.
3. And, somewhere in their list they will have bestsellers that do earn lots of money, and those will subsidise the rest. Unfortunately (or, from our point of view, fortunately), until it happens, they have no idea which titles those will be – so they have to continue to take on new authors and spread the net.

Thanks But No Thanks

So, no; thanks for the thought, but we will not split whatever the publisher coughs up. The author needs to pay the ghost a fair wage. What happens after that is, frankly, not the ghost's problem. Their job is to provide the text – and as it is a job, it can be paid for.

If the ghost really likes your project (or you), then they

might charge less than they would for another, similar job. Just because they charge full rate, don't assume they don't like your project (or you). The take home lesson: assume you're going to pay full rate, and if the ghost charges less then take it as a pleasant surprise.

For Ghostwriters: So, What Do I Charge?

It's a fact that sometimes you may have to think very hard about the job satisfaction to make up for the salary you know you could be earning in an office somewhere.

But you still need paying.

If you've been hired by a big publisher then they will probably have a budget for the title, and it will probably cover your requirements quite comfortably (though there's no harm in pushing a bit harder just to see what squeezes out). If this is a private job then you and the client need to work out a decent rate of payment between you – and it might not be easy.

I'm not going to specify figures because I hope this book will be around for a while, and I don't want to have to keep revising it, taking into account inflation and the cost of living. Your minimum requirement is that you are earning a living for the period that it takes you to do the work. And hopefully more.

So, in short:

- Calculate how long the job is likely to take you.

- Calculate how much of your annual income you need to earn in this period.
- Charge that.

I find a handy starting point is the National Union of Journalists' recommended rates (see 'Further Reading'). I'm not a member of the NUJ, but it's useful to quote because it has a certain clout and these are worked out by people who do this for a living every day. And I don't like to undercut the union. But again, there's no reason you can't quote higher if you think it's matching the quality of the work you are going to do.

EASING THE STING

If you or the client find the sum quoted still a bit high for comfort then you might be able to ease the sting if you also have other income streams coming in over this period, which means you can therefore adjust the rate for the book pro rata. That is your personal decision, though.

Once you have a sum in mind, you can ease the sting further by breaking it into instalments. Thirds is a popular option: on signature of the agreement; on delivery of the first draft; and on delivery of the final draft following author feedback. You could insert another stage at halfway to the deadline. This is all something else to be discussed between author and ghost – but it needs to happen.

And remember what it is you are charging for. I see no harm in giving a free consultation, like any good tradesman. That could be the initial discussion over Zoom. But any time taken to talk with a client is time you could be writing for someone else. If you have to travel to see them, at least work out an hourly rate, and the travel costs themselves. You might not just be writing the book; you may be plotting and outlining as well. It's all time taken. Only you know exactly what it is costing you – but it is costing something.

OTHER WAYS

Once I was hired to finish the second book of a two-book series: the client genuinely wrote the first one on his own (and very good it was too) but other professional commitments meant he simply didn't have time to finish the second. For payment he very kindly agreed I should receive the full advance he got from the publisher, as a flat fee. It constituted a very fair payment for the work I did, and I had absolutely no objections. I don't know how the series fared at the publisher or how sales went thereafter. That is not my problem. I had done my job and I had been paid; nuff said.

If the author is absolutely confident that their book will start earning the big bucks then you can write into your contract that the ghost's payment is itself an advance against proceeds from the publisher. But a payment there must be.

WHY YOU'RE WORTH IT

I personally think most people are prepared to pay professional rates for a professional job, though there are people who are only prepared to fork out bottom dollar for any kind of work. A friend used to live in the flat below one such person, who took it into his head to redecorate and do some other building work. His was a tale of endless renovations, because he would hire the cheapest workers he could find, fall out with them, sack them and then hire the next cheapest workers he could find to make do the bodged or incomplete work the first lot had done. My friend never asked the sums but we're both prepared to bet the neighbour paid a lot more over time than he would have if he had just paid a little extra to start with.

If you think hiring a professional is expensive, so the adage goes, try hiring an amateur.

One more good reason for being paid decently is that it gives you a contractual relationship with your client. I used to run my own publishing company and I learnt the hard way not to get work for free. I tried to work with people that I thought would share the vision and join me in working for peanuts or less. Some genuinely did share the vision but even they could be… well, flaky. Very good at their job but hard to pin down. They stuck to their own timetable, not to mine, and couldn't be pinned down to delivery dates. And why should they? They were doing me a favour so I was on their timetable. My work went straight to the back of the queue if something more remunerative and urgent came in.

And, it's two-way. If you're being paid then you are better able to tell if you're being taken for a ride, and to apportion your time for this task. If you find they're giving you too much work for the time paid, you have more leverage than if you're just doing them a favour.

For Both: PLR and ALCS

Two sets of initials that are there to help you: two sources of free, almost effortless money. Interested?

ALCS (The Authors' Licensing and Collecting Society) collects funds from licensed copying of authors' works, and disburses them to the creators. PLR (Public Lending Right), administered by the British Library, lets authors be paid every time one of their books is taken out of a library.

Both funds pay out once a year, and even though neither payment will be huge, they are both another item in the 'Better than a slap in the face with a wet fish' category.

But, both titles and authors need to be registered with both organisations for payments to be made, and both organisations require proof of your creative input. For the author, this is easy; their name is on the front cover. For the ghost, without a name on the cover, or at least a very obvious allusion to their role inside, this becomes harder; and if they officially don't exist, then it is of course impossible.

I have had professional contracts where quite simply I can't claim PLR or ALCS because I have no way of proving my contribution in a way that will satisfy them. (I console myself that the author probably doesn't know about them and I'm not going to be the one to tell them.) But it is still worth a try; and if yours is a private relationship then I see no reason at all why you shouldn't work something out that benefits both of you.

I've talked about these two funds here because 1) they also come under the heading of 'The Money' and 2) it paves the way for when I mention them later.

10. The Legal Side

The law is there for everyone. Use it.[30]

Get A Contract

Contracts! Do we really need them? Can't we do without? They sound so... binding. Ungentlemanly. Untrusting, even.

And essential.

A contract puts everything down in black and white. Who owes what to whom and by when. Both parties will need this.

Yes, both sides want to trust each other from the start – but if trust is already high then there should be no problem about writing it down, should there?

Here are some of the not-unknown scenarios that a contract protects against.

The ghost:

- ... falls ill and physically can't work for a couple of months.
- ... prefers to write undisturbed until the first draft is done, while the author wants to see weekly drafts.
- ... expected to see their name on the cover.
- ... wasn't expecting their name on the cover, but did think they would get a suitable acknowledgement.

---

30   Disclaimer: I'm not a lawyer, but disregard this section at your peril.

- … learns the book did so well that they start to feel that perhaps they were stiffed on the fee.
- … expected a share of the royalties, while the author thought they were paying a one-off fee.
- … expected to be paid in instalments rather than delivery.

The author:

- … thought they were paying on delivery rather than instalments.
- … suddenly introduces extra conditions for paying at each stage.
- … delays endlessly on checking the proofs, meaning that the ghost doesn't get paid the final instalment because it is contingent on author approval.
- … has bad luck on the horses and decides halfway through that actually they can't afford to pay what they agreed.
- … expects the ghost to just write the thing based on a few notes, and the ghost is rather hoping the author will provide a detailed outline.
- … dies, and their partner doesn't feel obliged to complete the book, or pay the ghost for work done.
- … dies, and their partner takes over the project and proceeds to reshape its requirements based on their own ideas – for no extra payment, of course.

If you have been brought together by a publisher or an agent then a contract will probably follow automatically; you still need to study it. If you are contracting as private individuals then the contract might be up to you both to sort out.

The UK's Society of Authors publishes a lot of advice and guidance, and (for members) a contract vetting service: see 'Further Reading'. But here are some of the things the contract should include.

- *The parties*. Exactly who is making this contract, with whom (including heirs and assigns), and to do what.
- *Payments*. Who pays what and how much...
- *Dates*. ...and by when. Also the defining stages of this project: when the author will commence work; when the first draft will be delivered by; how soon the author's comments will be received back by; when the author will deliver the final draft.
- *Termination*. The point that either party can withdraw from the contract altogether, if necessary, before the book is completed.
- *Libel*. You do *not* want to fall foul of the UK's libel laws, widely regarded as some of the most defendant-punitive and plaintiff-friendly in the world.

  In its simplest form, libel is a statement made in writing that is not only untrue but defamatory. Something like, 'Mr Brian Johnson of 123 Acacia Avenue, Everytown is an orophile', when he isn't, or at least there is no evidence that he is. If Mr Johnson has been found guilty in court of orophilia then fair enough; it's on the public record. Anything prior to that stage is potentially libellous, and the burden of proof will be on you both – author and ghost.

However, it's not always that simple. If Mr Brian Johnson recognises himself in your book's depiction of Mr Bryan Jolson of 123 Acorn Avenue, Everytown – or if he thinks others will – then he may still take action. And the burden will still fall on author and ghost to prove that no, honestly, you absolutely had no intention of libelling Mr Johnson.

There is a crumb of comfort in that the dead can't sue, and if Mr Johnson has since died then you may get away with it. But their family might still suffer distress, or maybe feel libelled at your implication that they colluded in his orophilia. And even a case that has no hope of succeeding must be fought and defended first.

So, the author must indemnify the ghost against anything they reveal subsequently being proved (or even suspected to be) libellous – and, the ghost must give the author the same protection against any material of their own that they use. After all, they might know just the real-life person to model an unpleasant character on, or have experienced just the right situation to rework for a piece of fiction. The author likes what they wrote and assumes they made it all up – until the writs start arriving. Libel law seeks to trap as many people as it can within its net, and without mutual indemnity, chances are good that both will end up paying.

- *Copyright*. Under UK law, anything written down is automatically copyrighted to the person doing the physical act of writing. This is so for shopping lists, to novels and anything else created in this way.

It also applies even if the writer is doing that writing for someone else – unless both parties have a contract which specifically releases that copyright. Copyright cannot be transferred orally on a gentleman's agreement.

The contract should not only cover this, but the future life of the work in any other form: translation rights, media adaptations or whatever.

- *Ownership*. Like copyright, if you write something then it is automatically yours, unless you stipulate otherwise in writing. Drafts, notes and other documents are also yours unless and until you transfer ownership. It doesn't matter that it's based on someone else's ideas.

So, everything that the ghost writes belongs to them, even if the author is paying them – until that ownership is contractually transferred.

Formal ownership of the text also protects both parties if the ghost dislikes what the author does with it. The author might mangle the published text so badly that the ghost thinks it reflects badly on their ability to string words together. With a contract, the ghost can publicly wash their hands of it – and, as the text is theirs, bought and paid for, the author has nothing to apologise for.

I told the story of the lady in the Introduction mostly from memory, because I've deleted our correspondence. We did not, at the time, have a contract, and so – technically – I was the owner both of the emails she had sent me, and the notes that I had made on her behalf. Even so, morally I felt it all belonged to her and I had no need to keep it. I sent her everything I had done and deleted my copies.

If in doubt, the moral position is often the best one to take.

NDAs

Non Disclosure Agreements are quite common in ghostwriting for non-fiction. Much of the information that passes through the ghost's hands could be very sensitive. Autobiographies, whistleblowing exposés, technical manuals, business books… They can all feature information which in the wrong hands, or released at the wrong time, could wreak havoc, or make someone or cost someone else a lot of money.

In fiction, though, NDAs are really not necessary.

BUT SOMEONE MIGHT STEAL MY IDEA!

… is the main worry of any client who inclines towards an NDA.

They won't.

First, an idea is by definition unstealable. Even if I told you, 'I'm going to write a novel about a Royal Navy in space', and you think that sounds interesting and you might have a go yourself, then I can pretty well guarantee that every image that is now passing through your mind is different to what passes through mine. And the end results will be as different as chalk and cheese.

Case in point: were I a clueless amateur, here is how I could, if I wanted, bring a case against a well-known and respected TV writer and producer.

Back in the mid-90s, Steven Moffat – now known for *Press Gang*, *Coupling*, *Doctor Who*, *Sherlock* and more – and I had consecutive stories in a themed *Doctor Who* anthology. Every story was linked to the one that came after it, so the authors needed to communicate beforehand to work out what the link should be. We chatted one night on the phone.

I have absolutely no memory of what we talked about, other than the stories. But. At the time, I was working on *His Majesty's Starship*. "So, what else are you working on?" he might have asked. "Oh, just a novel about the UK in space," I might have answered. "Oh?" he might have purred in his soft Scottish lilt. "Tell me more…"

And that might be how, fifteen years later, now writer and series producer for *Doctor Who,* Steven Moffat came to write an episode called 'The Beast Below' which features the UK in space…

Do I believe that?

No. Not for one second.

Even if I did, it wouldn't matter. His TV episode and my novel are very different in style, theme, plot and indeed subject matter. They are completely different entities, handling the whole idea of a UK in space in completely different ways.

Here's the thing: ideas can't be plagiarised. Which is lucky for me, as the inspiration for *His Majesty's Starship* was a throwaway line about the Royal Space Force in a Robert Heinlein novel.

So, How Does Plagiarism Work?

It is – probably, but I would still have to prove it – plagiarism if not only does Author A's novel's treatment of an idea seem very akin to the previously published Author B's, but it includes characters who are also strangely similar, and a plot with distinct elements of déjà vu, and even some sentences that are almost word for word identical. In such a case it might not be hard to make a case that Author A plagiarised Author B's book. They would obviously have gone to some lengths and effort to replicate someone else's work, and that is a crime.

Harvard student Kavya Viswanathan's debut novel *How Opal Mehta Got Kissed, Got Wild, and Got a Life* made enough of a splash to attract a two-book publishing deal and a movie deal – until it emerged that large chunks seemed to have been lifted direct from *Sloppy Firsts* and *Second Helpings*, two novels by Megan McCafferty, with only a little bit of tweaking to distinguish them. That *was* held to be plagiarism.

J.K. Rowling was accused of plagiarising the plot of *The Adventures of Willy the Wizard* by Adrian Jacobs (published 1997), a 36-page novel featuring a contest between wizards, for *Harry Potter and the Goblet of Fire* (published 2000), a door-stopping blockbuster which features a contest between wizards.[31] That was *not* held to be plagiarism. Quite apart from the fact that she had previously managed to write three bestselling novels without plundering *The Adventures of Willy the Wizard,* wizard contests are hardly that original

---

31   Another claimed common element was that both books feature wizards travelling on trains.

an idea. Lawyers for the estates of J.R.R. Tolkien and Ursula K. Le Guin were signally not reaching for their quills.

In 'What Makes A Good Ghostwriter?' I mentioned the lady whose ghostwriter stole a chapter from David Gemmell. That *was* plagiarism, though as far as I'm aware the Gemmell estate didn't lower itself to getting involved.

But, I repeat, the idea cannot be stolen.

BUT, BUT...

In fact, this is how fiction develops. Authors pick up other authors' ideas, and run with them.

Yes, but that's just inspiration. Someone might steal my exact idea!

Why?

If a ghostwriter or agent or publisher thinks an idea, as is, could make a huge amount of money then why would they steal it from you and give it to someone else to write? Why not just let you write it and cut out the middleman?

But, let's be frank: I'm no one, just a beginner. No one will read my book, but in the hands of a more marketable author it could be a bestseller!

And those more marketable authors – read: experienced, been around the block, know what they're doing – are incapable of coming up with good ideas of their own? How do you think they became marketable in the first place? It was not by pinching ideas off other aspiring writers; it was by hard work and being very good at what they do.

A story isn't just about the idea – see 'How Fiction Works', if you haven't already. A story is the idea and the characters and the writing and the plot and the words and the style and the imagery – all the things that make it unique. All the things that make it the story you want to tell.

11. Conclusion

So, there you have it.

If you have newly joined the ghostwriting fraternity, or are thinking of doing so, then congratulations! It is a worthy profession. You have the power to release more quality fiction into the world, and that can only be a good thing.

And if you're thinking of getting a ghostwriter, you should now be in a position to make an informed decision, eyes open, aware of all the benefits and all the pitfalls ahead. This will not be just dumping a job on to someone else's shoulders and stepping back. It will be a collaboration, everyone playing to their strengths, and it will be a very rewarding one.

My personal hope is that you will go for it, and not just because I enjoy earning money, not starving and being able to heat my home in the cold weather. I like good books. I like fiction. Fiction is where the ideas that can change the world begin. The world needs more fiction. I hope you will go back to that idea at the back of a drawer, dust it off, have a look… and get in touch to see how a ghostwriter can make it work.

Appendix 1

What Do I Do With My Manuscript?

Strictly speaking, this is beyond the remit of this book, but it's something a lot of authors want to know. Let's assume you have decided to engage the services of a ghostwriter. Well done!

But, once you finally have that manuscript in your hands, once the idea that has consumed you for so long is there in front of you in black and white, for you to do with as you will…

What exactly will you do with it?

Lewis Carroll again:

> *Then proudly smiled that old man*
> *To see the eager lad*
> *Rush madly for his pen and ink*
> *And for his blotting-pad –*
> *But, when he thought of publishing,*
> *His face grew stern and sad.*

Once your ghostwriter has delivered your masterpiece, you presumably will want people to read it. It could just be for friends and family, so you could just print it out or email it to them. But I will assume you would like to see it made more widely available, buyable in bookshops and listed on Amazon.

For the sake of argument, I will describe two options: finding a traditional publisher, or self-publishing.

Once again there are a lot of BOCTAOEs in what follows.

Should I Find A Traditional Publisher?

The attractions of a traditional publisher are obvious. For a start, you get money up front in the form of an advance. And – in principle at least – they do all the work of marketing it. (Though I warn you now, you will be expected to do a lot yourself.)

You knew there was a 'but' coming, didn't you?

The competition is almost overwhelming. Publishers are deluged with submissions. For that reason they will very likely accept submissions only from agents; that way, if a manuscript reaches their desk then at least it has already been filtered by at least one pair of eyes. Someone has already thought it might be worth taking a punt on.

But agents are even more deluged. The number of submissions a week from prospective clients will be in the double figures, and in a year, they might take on only two or three of them.

And even once you are in through the door, don't expect the riches to start flowing. This is what the lady in the Introduction just couldn't get. See the chapter on 'The Money' for why. Margins are now so thin in publishing that, the bigger and richer the publisher, the more likely it seems to prefer books by established names that it knows will sell. These, hopefully, will subsidise the rest of their books.

But that means that they are very, very picky about that 'rest of'.

So, even if your book gets through the door and even if it lands on an editor's desk, the journey isn't over. Your book will have to pass through a barrage of readers, all of whom will look at it from a different angle and all of whom will have to give it the thumbs-up. All of whom must agree that yes, this is worth spending a (small) sum of money on.

But, there is hope. Authors are picking up on the fact that it is more and more up to them to sell their own books. As a result, they are getting more and more independent. Which brings me inevitably on to:

Should I Self-Publish?

The advantages of self-publishing are obvious. You have complete creative control of the project, and after expenses have been paid, you get to keep every penny of the proceeds.

The nature of self-publishing, and the fact that it's usually easier to sell books as part of a series than stand-alone, means it is especially helpful for genre fiction – science fiction and fantasy, romance, crime. The romance category is almost completely independent by now, and there are probably more high earning self-published genre authors than traditionally published. Genres have their own built-in audiences, which the algorithms of the various online selling machines can sniff out and push your book at.

THE DRAWBACKS

But, you need to do EVERYTHING. Stop and think about the implications of that for a moment.

- *Book design:* you need to get it typeset and a nice cover made up.
- *Developmental editing / structural editing / copy editing* (see 'How Fiction Works'): yes, all your responsibility too.
- *Marketing:* Amazon, Lulu etc. have their own little mechanisms to help you along here but the responsibility is on you to make it work. You must keep on top of it every step of the way. I do personally know people who earn a living from self-publishing – but usually this involves setting aside at least one day every week just for the marketing.

And – despite what I was just saying about the algorithms and the inbuilt audiences – you might have to try even harder to get noticed in the first place. If you can be published by a traditional publisher, the reader at least knows your book passed through a number of professional processes to make the story as polished and gripping as it can be. Even a well-written first draft will be immeasurably improved by the time it emerges into bookshops. Self-publishers, it can't be denied, have a tendency to skimp on those stages, or aren't even aware that they are needed. The end result is inevitably not as good as it would be from a traditional publisher and your book can be swamped by the lower-quality book product.

But, this does not have to be so. All those stages are available to you too – if you are prepared to pay for them. That pile of profits you're looking forward to might start to diminish in front of your eyes as you do the sums.

AND IF SO, WHO WITH?

We really are getting beyond the remit now. I will leave the joy of investigating the options offered by reputable outfits like Lulu.com, IngramSpark and Amazon KDP to you.

Other Options

There are other options, like serial novels, or whipping up money through Kickstarter or Patreon or Substack. This is outside my experience and I can't really comment – though I commend Elle Griffin's thoughts (see 'Further Reading').

Appendix 2

A Sample Contract

If you have been hired by a company or agent, they will probably have their own standard contract. It is still worth checking to see that the points here are covered. They might put their foot down and say, "No", but hey, you tried. Hopefully you're being paid enough to make it worthwhile.

If yours is a private arrangement then you can tweak all this to your heart's content.

Once again, I cannot stress enough how much I am not a lawyer, and once again I point you at the Society of Authors' legal help page.

AGREEMENT

1. This agreement is made between **[author's name]** and their heirs and assigns ('AUTHOR') and **[your name]** ('GHOSTWRITER') concerning work on a manuscript provisionally titled **[book's name]** ('the Book').

[**BJ:** You can include your addresses if you like but it is probably not necessary.]

2. GHOSTWRITER is hired to write a draft of approximately **[insert book length]** words.

3. GHOSTWRITER will develop the plot line, chapter outline, list of characters and any other supporting material for the Book in collaboration with AUTHOR.

[**BJ:** Just how closely you collaborate is between the two of you, but the author needs to know they have some responsibility here. Of course, the author might already have a pretty good idea about these items; they may even supply it all up front.]

4. AUTHOR will have the final say on the text of the Book.

5. GHOSTWRITER will not disclose to any third party anything learnt or revealed during the writing of the Book that is not already in the public domain.

INDEMNITY

6. AUTHOR warrants and undertakes that their contribution to the Book shall be wholly original and that such contribution shall not infringe the copyright or other intellectual property rights or other rights of any third party, or to the best of AUTHOR's knowledge be obscene or defamatory of any person. AUTHOR will indemnify GHOST against any liability arising from a breach of this warranty.

7. GHOST warrants and undertakes that their contribution to the Book shall be wholly original save to the extent that it derives from AUTHOR's contribution and that GHOST's contribution shall not infringe the copyright or other intellectual property rights or other rights of any third party or to the best

of GHOST's knowledge be obscene or defamatory of any person. GHOST will indemnify AUTHOR and any publisher against any liability arising from a breach of this warranty.

TERMINATION

8. Either party has the right to terminate this agreement on written notice to the other at any time. On termination, any amounts outstanding for the work carried out to the date of termination shall become immediately payable.

CREDIT, COPYRIGHT AND OWNERSHIP

9. Credit for the Book will fall to AUTHOR.

[**BJ:** Though, if the author is happy for your name to go on the cover too – perhaps in smaller print, or perhaps proudly as co-author – then that's great.]

10. Copyright and all other rights in the Book will reside with AUTHOR.

11. Ownership of the final text of the Book, all drafts and all resources used in the preparation of the Book (notes, chapter outlines, etc.) together with all right, title and interest in any intellectual property created by GHOST on AUTHOR's behalf will reside with AUTHOR.

12. GHOST hereby waives all moral rights in the Book as defined by the Copyright Designs and Patents Act 1988 and any equivalent rights in any jurisdiction.

13. On delivery of the final draft of the Book, or

upon termination of this agreement, GHOST will return to AUTHOR or destroy all materials, or copies thereof, any transcripts or recordings of interviews between AUTHOR and GHOST and any other preparatory materials for the Book.

ACKNOWLEDGMENT

14. AUTHOR will give GHOSTWRITER an acknowledgment in the Acknowledgments section of the Book.

[**BJ:** You could if you like specify a wording that will make the ghost's contribution clear, at least to the cognoscenti. Perhaps something like "Thanks to [ghostwriter's name] for all the words." Remember that you want to prove eligibility for PLR and ALCS.]

ROYALTIES

15. GHOSTWRITER will not be entitled to any royalties, residuals, or commissions from AUTHOR, their publisher or agents upon the sale of the Book or upon sale of any rights in the Book.

[**BJ:** If you can work out a royalty deal, of course, then so much the better. You could, by mutual arrangement, work out a deal such that the fee paid by the author is an advance against what they get from the publisher; in other words, publisher revenue is split on a percentage which you will also specify here, but only once your advance has been paid off. But, do not let this replace being paid an actual fee.]

16. AUTHOR will register the Book with the British Library for Public Lending Right (PLR), and with the The Authors' Licensing and Collecting Society (ALCS). Payments from PLR and ALCS will be divided between AUTHOR and GHOST on the basis of **[insert the percentages you work out here]**.

[BJ: Look, it's worth a try.]

TIMESCALE

17. Total payment for GHOSTWRITER made by by AUTHOR is payable according to the terms listed below.

18. GHOSTWRITER will deliver the first draft of the Book by **[insert date].**

[**BJ:** Or, within [insert period] of commencement of work.]

19. AUTHOR will provide detailed feedback on the draft within **[insert number]** weeks of receipt of the draft.

20. AUTHOR will provide the final draft of the Book within **[insert number]** weeks of receipt of the feedback.

21. At any stage, AUTHOR will respond to queries from GHOSTWRITER within **[insert a time period]**.

[**BJ:** 48 hours works for me.]

22. GHOSTWRITER and AUTHOR will each let the other know as soon as possible of any likely delays in this timescale.

Payment

23. AUTHOR will pay GHOSTWRITER the total sum of **[insert sum]**, to be delivered in stages as follows upon receipt of invoice from GHOSTWRITER:

- 25% on signature of this agreement and commencement of work.
- 25% at the projected midway point between commencement of work and delivery of the first draft of the Book.
- 25% on delivery of the first draft of the Book.
- 25% on AUTHOR's approval of the final draft of the Book.

[**BJ:** Work out the stages that suit you best, but these are good ones. If you've negotiated payment as per clause 15, this is the time to say so.]

24. This agreement shall be governed by English law and the parties submit to the exclusive jurisdiction of the courts of England and Wales.

[**BJ:** Even Brits often forget that the different parts of the United Kingdom have subtly different laws. If you and the author live in different areas, or the author lives abroad, you will need to stipulate the area you have in mind.]

This agreement is concluded by:

[author's name]   **[your name]**

Date: Date:

APPENDIX 3

Scams, And How
To Avoid Them

If you decide to self-publish then one unavoidable drawback is that it paints a large target on your back for those who would prey on the weak and vulnerable. You will be perceived as a clueless newbie and so the predators will come crawling out of the woodwork.

And they might do that anyway, even if you're traditionally published.

Some important resources that I recommend you use:

- *Writer Beware:* a free service that exists to ferret out and reveal information about literary scams and unethical behaviour. Operated by Science Fiction Writers of America but applicable to any genre.
- *Whois:* a free web service that lets you look up the details of any website.
- A nakedly suspicious mind about anything that looks too good to be true.

ANATOMY OF A SCAM

An email I recently received:

> *This is* [name pinched from a genuine bona fide literary agent] *from* [made-up agency name]. *This is to inform you that we received a call from Traditional Publishing Company. They made an initial evaluation about your book entitled "The Teen, the Witch & the Thief" and they're interested in the Book Acquisition Project.*
>
> *I'm not sure if you realize it but you have a very good material and at the same time you were able to catch the attention of Literary Agents.*
>
> *I'd like to know the best time to talk so we can discuss how we can make things happen. You can reply to this email or you can call me with my number.*

Take it from me, the only genuine thing there is the name of my book. How do I know the rest is a scam?

1. Literary agents don't solicit out of the blue.
2. If a publisher really was interested in acquiring my novel, they would contact me direct.
3. In the unlikely event of a literary agent contradicting my first point and soliciting out of the blue, they would do it in coherent English.
4. And anyway, in the first paragraph they said a publisher had noticed my book; in the second, suddenly it's been noticed by a literary agent. Sorry, Literary Agent.
5. 'Traditional Publishing Company'? Oh, please. It could be the name of an actual company, but it's such a generic phrase it's almost impossible to do a search on. Given the rest of the email, it's more

likely the author hasn't heard of indefinite articles, and doesn't realise that you don't capitalise phrases Just Because They're Important.

6. This is the funniest bit. 'I'm not sure if you realise it but you have a very good material…' (Well, frankly, I did have an inkling it might be, which is why I wrote it and got it published. But thanks for the affirmation.) '… and at the same time you were able to catch the attention of Literary Agents.' Because the two – very good material, and snagging an agent's attention – are usually so incompatible?

7. You will have to take my word for this as I'm not publicising them, but if you went to their website, you would find the staff pictures all use the names of genuine members of the publishing industry, all of whom (a simple Google search shows) work in other companies. The staff pictures are stock poses pinched from the Pexels image library. (You knew you can search for images as well on Google… didn't you?) Also, according to Whois, while these people claim on their website to have been in operation for 20+ years, their website was first registered 20+ days before I received this email.

I will concede that they did two things right. One was to email me direct; very often, with an email like this you will see that you are just one of an unknown quantity of BCC'd recipients. The other was that they actually named one of my books. Far more common is a generic reference to 'your book'. They assume you only have one, or they are hoping you will jump to an immediate conclusion as to which of your titles they are talking about.

What If...?

What would have happened if I had nibbled their bait?

They would have charged money to take me on as a client to represent me to Traditional Publishing Company and then, most likely, simply disappeared. In the vanishingly small possibility that they really would have tried to sell my book to another company, I would have ended up paying through the nose for an inferior, badly produced product that wasn't half as good as the existing product I made myself with the help of a little basic typesetting and the services of Amazon KDP.

How do I all know this?

Because it's an old, old story. Sharks circling the small fish in the pond. Chancers hoping that because you are self-published, you are ipso facto an innocent abroad, desperate for the respectability of a professional publishing deal and hopefully bigger money than you are currently getting. I cannot strongly enough recommend Writer Beware, which exists exactly to ferret out people like this.

I'm aware there has been a lot of negativity in this Appendix, especially perhaps in the last bit. None of this needs to be an obstacle to you achieving your dream of telling your story, and getting people to read it. Your basic defences against this kind of thing: knowledge; Google; Whois; Writer Beware; and, best of all, professionalism and common sense.

You're welcome.

APPENDIX 4

The Obligatory Origin Story

I got here purely by accident. This is not uncommon among ghostwriters. I know many people who have always wanted to write, and I know a few who have never done anything else but write, and I know several ghostwriters – but I don't know any ghostwriter who never thought of doing anything else. Ghostwriting is no one's Plan A. It's something that creeps up on you, takes you by surprise – and then you realise this is clearly where you were meant to be.

Everyone's story is different, but this is mine.

THE WILDERNESS YEARS

I had the good fortune to cut my writing teeth in the world of science fiction, a genre with a well developed critical field and a very democratic approach to writers. It is receptive to new voices, encouraging to anyone who feels like putting pen to paper with thoughts of their own, and very quick to let you know how you might improve.

I started writing after my A-levels, just to get rid of the ideas crowding in my head. As a student I discovered the magazine *Interzone,* which was then just about the only UK market for short science fiction stories. And so I bombarded them with stories, which at first were invariably rejected. But – because the editorial team were wonderful people, and had all been in my situation themselves – I usually got at least a couple of lines of feedback. I paid attention, and incorporated what they were saying, and got to the stage of being good enough to get several lines of feedback in the rejections. The *Interzone* editors weren't afraid to suggest alternative markets for stories they turned down, and so my first actual fiction sale was to the anthology *Digital Dreams* (NEL 1990), edited by David V. Barrett and carrying stories by authors who included Terry Pratchett, Neil Gaiman... and some bloke called Jeapes.

Meanwhile, at some time during my struggling years of jumping up and down and shouting, "I'm a writer, notice me," I heard of Milford and I immediately knew I wanted to go.

Milford is an annual science fiction and fantasy writers' workshop. The minimum credential for entering is that you have to have made a professional sale – no absolute beginners. Once a year, a small group of writers congregate for a week, and everyone submits an unpublished piece of work that everyone else reads and then critiques. When your turn comes up, everyone gets two minutes to say their piece, while you bite your tongue and sit on your hands and don't say a word. Then you get two minutes to deliver your response. Then everyone else gets a further minute to come back to your comeback. Then it all breaks down into general chat, conversation and tea and biscuits until the next story comes up for discussion.

And in between you talk writing, eat and breathe

writing, live writing. It is the best thing that can happen to anyone wanting to be a writer.

Entry is by invitation only. I didn't know David Barrett had put me, and every other first time author in *Digital Dreams*, on the invitation list until I got my invitation to Milford 1991. It was everything I hoped for – and as well as making some lifelong friends, some of those new friends invited me to join their writer's group.

YOU SOLD IT TO WHO?

Meanwhile, out in the real world, I had a day job. I didn't know much about writing but I knew enough to know I would need an actual job to live off. I never expected writing to make me more than pocket money. As it was, I found myself in a company that published academic journals and a monthly newspaper for the information industry, *Information World Review*. Even though I was only hired as a copy editor to start with, the new publishing director was happy to teach me the basics of journalism and technical writing, so I became an occasional reporter and columnist too. Within a few years my writing CV included both fiction and non-fiction, which is a handy place to be.

Back at the writer's group, several of my friends there already had an agent. The agent was so impressed by what he heard of the rest of us that he asked anyone else who wrote a novel to give him first refusal.

Which I duly did with my first novel, *His Majesty's Starship*.

This was where things got very unexpected. He sold it… to Scholastic. I had written what I thought was a perfectly good grown-up science fiction book – the hero was a depressive middle-aged divorcee and it even had some alien sex in it – and he sold it to a bloody children's publisher.

Which turned out to be the best thing that ever happened to me, because it meant that quite by accident, I became a children's author.

THE ACCIDENTAL GHOST

Fast forward a few years. I was in circumstances where I was rapidly running out of money and I wanted something – anything, within my skill set – that would earn some. A friend suggested Working Partners. As Sebastian Rook, I found myself writing the first three novels of *The Vampire Plagues*, which kept me financially afloat for a couple of years until I could gratefully go back to full-time work.

I was now a documentation officer for a computer network. My job was meant to be editing and publishing technical reports and other material, which were all written by people far busier and cleverer than me. However, because they were far busier and cleverer than me, they didn't have time to write the things. It turned out to be easier all round if I interviewed them and then wrote the material myself. So, suddenly I was ghostwriting without even realising it, and in that way I accidentally became a technical writer too. And discovered I quite enjoyed it.

Meanwhile, my Working Partners editor, Amber Caraveo, changed jobs and inherited a series of young adult adventures by a well-known celebrity whose name I am not officially allowed to divulge – so just call him Client Zero.

The series needed a ghostwriter, and because Amber had enjoyed working with me in the past she thought of me now.

I've described my growing involvement with Client Zero elsewhere in this book. What I didn't mention was that when his agents got in touch about a third series, they added that he was parting ways with his publisher and was going to publish the new series through his own company. This would require someone not just to write it but to plan and plot it too. It was a four-book series to be written over the course of a year, and the extra work entailed meant that the pay equated to a year's salary from my then employer. So, I left and never looked back. That was 2015.

So, that's my origin story. The moral: expect the unexpected, grab opportunities, and don't be a pain in the backside to work with.

FURTHER READING

[Douglas Adams]

> *The Salmon of Doubt: Hitchhiking the Galaxy One Last Time.* Pan 2021.

[Scott Adams]

> **https://dilbert.com/** [retrieved 3rd September 2024].

[ALCS]

> **https://www.alcs.co.uk/** [retrieved 3rd September 2024].

[ChatGPT]

> 'ChatGPT: US lawyer admits using AI for case research'. BBC News. **https://www.bbc.co.uk/news/world-us-canada-65735769** [retrieved 3rd September 2024].

[Lewis Carroll]

> 'Poeta Fit, Non Nascitur'. Full text at **https://www.online-literature.com/carroll/2822/** [retrieved 3rd September 2024].

[Neil Clarke]

> 'A Concerning Trend'. **https://neil-clarke.com/a-concerning-trend/** [retrieved 3rd September 2024].

[Graham Greene]

> 'Graham Greene', by Julian Evans. **https://www.prospectmagazine.co.uk/essays/56572/graham-greene** [retrieved 3rd September 2024].

[Elle Griffin]

> 'Writing Books Isn't A Good Idea'. **https://www.elysian.press/p/creator-economy-for-fiction-authors** [retrieved 3rd September 2024].

'No One Buys Books'. **https://www.elysian.press/p/no-one-buys-books** [retrieved 3rd September 2024].

'You will not make money from your Patreon or Substack platform'. **https://www.elysian.press/i/34068497/you-will-not-make-money-from-your-patreon-or-substack-platform** [retrieved 3rd September 2024].

[A.C. Hilton]

'The Vulture and the Husbandman'. Full text at **https://allpoetry.com/The-Vulture-and-the-Husbandman** [retrieved 3rd September 2024].

[Juliet E. McKenna]

'How To Be Original and Still Get Published'. **https://www.julietemckenna.com/other/how-to-be-original-and-still-get-published/** [retrieved 3rd September 2024].

[Somerset Maugham]

I have found the quote at the start of 'How Fiction Works' attributed to Maugham in many places on the net; so many that I've been unable to pinpoint the exact source.

[Minimum wage]

https://www.moneysavingexpert.com/family/national-minimum-wage [retrieved 3rd September 2024].

[Net Book Agreement]

https://en.wikipedia.org/wiki/Net_Book_Agreement [retrieved 3rd September 2024].

[NUJ]

https://www.londonfreelance.org/feesguide/index.php?&section=Print+media&subsect=Books&subsubs=Al [retrieved 3rd September 2024].

GHOSTWRITING NOVELS

[Andrew O'Hagan]

> 'Ghosting'. *London Review of Books*, Vol. 36, No. 5, 6th March 2014. https://www.lrb.co.uk/the-paper/v36/n05/andrew-o-hagan/ghosting [retrieved 3rd September 2024].

[George Orwell]

> The full text of *Nineteen Eighty-Four* is available at http://gutenberg.net.au/ebooks01/0100021.txt [retrieved 3rd September 2024].

[Plagiarism]

> Jim Macdonald, 'Weirdly Similar…'. Making Light. https://nielsenhayden.com/makinglight/archives/009448.html [retrieved 3rd September 2024].

> Dinitia Smith, 'Harvard Novelist Says Copying Was Unintentional', New York Times, 25 April 2014. https://www.nytimes.com/2006/04/25/books/harvard-novelist-says-copying-was-unintentional.html [retrieved 3rd September 2024].

> 'JK Rowling 'plagiarism' case fails.' BBC News. https://www.bbc.co.uk/news/entertainment-arts-14187849 [retrieved 3rd September 2024].

[Terry Pratchett]

> Terry Pratchett, 'Advice to Booksellers'. *A Slip of the Keyboard*. Corgi 2014.

[Public Lending Right]

> https://plr.bl.uk/login [retrieved 3rd September 2024].

[Salaries]

> https://uk.indeed.com/career/office-worker/salaries [retrieved 3rd September 2024].

[Ian Shircore]

'Royalties for commoners'. **https://www.unitedghostwriters.co.uk/ royalties-for-commoners/** [retrieved 3rd September 2024].

[Society of Authors]

'Advice: Contracts, fees, negotiations and more – explore our resources and ask for advice'. **https://www2.societyofauthors.org/ advice/** [retrieved 3rd September 2024].

'Artificial Intelligence: Protecting copyright and creative careers in the face of new technology'. **https://www2.societyofauthors.org/ where-we-stand/artificial-intelligence/** [retrieved 3rd September 2024].

[Margaret Thatcher]

'Margaret Thatcher 'didn't get Monty Python's dead parrot gag'. **https://www.independent.co.uk/news/people/margaret-thatcher-didn-t-get-monty-python-s-dead-parrot-gag-a6680081.html** [retrieved 3rd September 2024].

'Margaret Thatcher Recites Monty Python's Dead Parrot Sketch'. **https://www.youtube.com/watch?v=w5zfFWCaPOo** [retrieved 3rd September 2024].

[Whois]

https://whois.domaintools.com/ [retrieved 3rd September 2024].

[Writer Beware]

https://www.sfwa.org/other-resources/for-authors/writer-beware/ [retrieved 3rd September 2024].

[John Wyndham]

'Consider Her Ways'. **https://en.wikipedia.org/wiki/Consider_Her_ Ways** [retrieved 3rd September 2024].

ACKNOWLEDGEMENTS

Thank you to: beta readers Josh Bray, Ginny Carter, Gary Dalkin, Emma Darwin, David Griffiths, Jon Oliver, Simon Rae and Ralph Turner for many helpful suggestions; Liz Carter for the excellent cover; and Nick Mould for a bang-up job of proof reading. Any mistakes that crept in after his checking are my own fault.

THE AUTHOR

Ben Jeapes took up writing in the mistaken belief that it would be easier than a real job. It isn't, so he has been a book publisher, journal editor and technical writer as well as the author of eight novels and co-author of many more that annoyingly make much more money than his own. He is also the author of a children's biography of Ada Lovelace, and his published short stories are collected together in *Jeapes Japes*.

www.benjeapes.com

www.oxfordghostwriter.com

benjeapes.substack.com

If you enjoyed this book, why not take five minutes to leave a review on Amazon? The more reviews a book gets, the more the algorithms notice it and the more likely it is to get into the hands of someone else who might enjoy it.

Reviews don't have to be grammatical and spelt correctly. They don't have to be coherent or make sense. They don't even have to be positive. Amazon doesn't grade them. It just counts them.

Reviews really do make a difference.